Pomona College
Claremont, California

Written by Peter Cook

*Edited by Adam Burns, Kristen Burns,
and Jon Skindzier*

Layout by Alyson Pope

*Additional contributions by Omid Gohari,
Christina Koshzow, Chris Mason, Joey Rahimi,
and Luke Skurman*

ISBN # 1-4274-0112-8
ISSN # 1551-0625

Last updated 5/16/06

Special Thanks To: Babs Carryer, Andy Hannah, LaunchCyte, Tim O'Brien, Bob Sehlinger, Thomas Emerson, Andrew Skurman, Barbara Skurman, Bert Mann, Dave Lehman, Daniel Faycock, Chris Babyak, The Donald H. Jones Center for Entrepreneurship, Terry Slease, Jerry McGinnis, Bill Ecenberger, Idie McGinty, Kyle Russel, Jacque Zaremba, Larry Winderbaum, Roland Allen, Jon Reider, Team Evankovich, Lauren Varacalli, Abu Noaman, Mark Exler, Daniel Steinmeyer, Jared Cohon, Gabriela Oates, David Koegler, and Glen Meakem.

Bounce-Back Team: Lilas Harley, Colin Platt, and Christopher Cumming.

College Prowler®
5001 Baum Blvd.
Suite 750
Pittsburgh, PA 15213

Phone: 1-800-290-2682
Fax: 1-800-772-4972
E-Mail: info@collegeprowler.com
Web Site: www.collegeprowler.com

Welcome to College Prowler®

During the writing of College Prowler's guidebooks, we felt it was critical that our content was unbiased and unaffiliated with any college or university. We think it's important that our readers get honest information and a realistic impression of the student opinions on any campus—that's why if any aspect of a particular school is terrible, we (unlike a campus brochure) intend to publish it. While we do keep an eye out for the occasional extremist—the cheerleader or the cynic—we take pride in letting the students tell it like it is. We strive to create a book that's as representative as possible of each particular campus. Our books cover both the good and the bad, and whether the survey responses point to recurring trends or a variation in opinion, these sentiments are directly and proportionally expressed through our guides.

College Prowler guidebooks are in the hands of students throughout the entire process of their creation. Because you can't make student-written guides without the students, we have students at each campus who help write, randomly survey their peers, edit, layout, and perform accuracy checks on every book that we publish. From the very beginning, student writers gather the most up-to-date stats, facts, and inside information on their colleges. They fill each section with student quotes and summarize the findings in editorial reviews. In addition, each school receives a collection of letter grades (A through F) that reflect student opinion and help to represent contentment, prominence, or satisfaction for each of our 20 specific categories. Just as in grade school, the higher the mark the more content, more prominent, or more satisfied the students are with the particular category.

Once a book is written, additional students serve as editors and check for accuracy even more extensively. Our bounce-back team—a group of randomly selected students who have no involvement with the project—are asked to read over the material in order to help ensure that the book accurately expresses every aspect of the university and its students. This same process is applied to the 200-plus schools College Prowler currently covers. Each book is the result of endless student contributions, hundreds of pages of research and writing, and countless hours of hard work. All of this has led to the creation of a student information network that stretches across the nation to every school that we cover. It's no easy accomplishment, but it's the reason that our guides are such a great resource.

When reading our books and looking at our grades, keep in mind that every college is different and that the students who make up each school are not uniform—as a result, it is important to assess schools on a case-by-case basis. Because it's impossible to summarize an entire school with a single number or description, each book provides a dialogue, not a decision, that's made up of 20 different topics and hundreds of student quotes. In the end, we hope that this guide will serve as a valuable tool in your college selection process. Enjoy!

OMID GOHARI ○ CHRISTINA KOSHZOW ○ CHRIS MASON ○ JOEY RAHIMI ○ LUKE SKURMAN ○
The College Prowler Team

POMONA COLLEGE

Table of Contents

Introduction from the Author

Attention! Pomona College is not for everyone. If your goal in attending college is to rocket up the corporate ladder as quickly as possible, I suggest you put this book down right now. Maybe you should see if you can get your money back, as well. Pomona is, don't get me wrong, an excellent school. It's ranked right up there among liberal arts schools with Swarthmore and Amherst. The student store sells T-shirts which say "Harvard, the Pomona of the East," which is sort of funny, because a lot of people at Pomona tried to get into Harvard and couldn't. The shirts used to say "Pomona, the Harvard of the West," which is kind of sad if you think about it, and definitely speaks to the frustrations and insecurities that go hand in hand with attending one of the most selective and highly-ranked colleges in the country. The newer shirts are far cooler. Also, their ironic casualness speaks to a growing confidence that Pomona's students, alumni, faculty, and administrators have in the quality of their school.

The aura of confidence at Pomona is justifiably placed. Pomona has consistently climbed the college ratings year after year. It's well managed, has an enormous endowment, excellent faculty, a strong alumni network, and draws some of the finest students in the country. What then is the major difference between a place like Pomona and a place like Amherst? In one word, attitude. Pomona is anything but uptight, and the school's overall psyche is about as cutthroat as a game of Go Fish. Pomona consistently boasts one of the highest rankings for the country's happiest students.

It was a wise man who once said "with great power comes great responsibility." Well, if knowledge is power, then your average Pomona student has a lot more clout than most people their age. What they don't have, it seems, is responsibility. You're more likely to find Pomona students tanning at the pool (in the dead of winter, no less) rather than cramming in the library. That's the SoCal lifestyle. Many Pomona students spend their nights drinking as opposed to thinking. So, when does all the serious academic work get done? It's a mystery and, like most great mysteries, is better left unsolved. Suffice it to say that the work does get done.

So, in many ways, a Pomona education is a trade-off. Some pinch-browed, grumpy, overworked, over-caffeinated, under-rested, ulcer-plagued, miserable Amherst graduate may be a lot more likely to land a choice job right out of college. However, you will have a hard time convincing the tanned, relaxed Pomona student who is lounging, seemingly carefree, at the pool, drink in one hand, Aristotle in the other, that his or her straw is actually the shorter one.

It's hard to argue with contentment and happiness, and Pomona offers a far better than average shot at both. Oh, and lest I forget, you'll get an awfully good education as well.

Peter Cook, Author
Pomona College

By the Numbers

General Information

Pomona College
333 North College Way
Claremont, California 91711

Control:
Private

Academic Calendar:
Semester

Religious Affiliation:
None

Founded:
1887

Web Site:
www.pomona.edu

Main Phone:
(909) 621-8000

Admissions Phone:
(909) 621-8134

Student Body

**Full-Time
Undergraduates:**
1,559

**Part-Time
Undergraduates:**
0

**Total Male
Undergraduates:**
778

**Total Female
Undergraduates:**
781

Admissions

Overall Acceptance Rate:
20%

**Early Decision
Acceptance Rate:**
31%

Regular Acceptance Rate:
19%

Total Applicants:
4,927

Total Acceptances:
970

Freshman Enrollment:
394

**Yield (% of admitted
students who actually enroll):**
41%

Early Decision Available?
Yes

Early Action Available?
No

Early Decision Deadline:
November 15

Early Decision Notification:
December 15

Regular Decision Deadline:
January 2

**Regular Decision
Notification:**
April 10

Must-Reply-By Date:
May 1

**Applicants Placed on
Waiting List:**
0

**Transfer Applications
Recieved:**
200

**Transfer Applications
Accepted:**
19

Transfer Students Enrolled:
11

**Transfer Application
Acceptance Rate:**
1%

**Common Application
Accepted?**
Yes

Supplemental Forms?
Yes

Admissions E-Mail:
admissions@pomona.edu

Admissions Web Site:
www.pomona.edu/Admissions/
Home.shtml

SAT I or ACT Required?
Either

➜

**SAT I Range
(25th–75th Percentile):**
1370–1530

**SAT I Verbal Range
(25th–75th Percentile):**
690–770

**SAT I Math Range
(25th–75th Percentile):**
680–760

**Top 10% of
High School Class:**
86%

Retention Rate:
98%

Application Fee:
$60

Financial Information

Full-Time Tuition:
$29,923

Room and Board:
$10,851

Books and Supplies:
$850

**Avgerage Need-Based
Financial Aid Package
(including loans, work-study,
grants, and other sources):**
$27,866

**Students Who Applied for
Financial Aid:**
60%

**Students Who
Received Aid:**
53%

Financial Aid Forms Deadline:
February 1

Financial Aid Phone:
(909) 621-8205

Financial Aid E-Mail:
financial_aid@Pomona.edu

Financial Aid Web Site:
www.pomona.edu/financialaid

Academics

The Lowdown On...
Academics

Degrees Awarded:
Bachelor

Most Popular Majors:
13% Economics
 8% Biology
 8% English
 7% Political Science
 7% Psychology

Full-Time Faculty:
161

Faculty with Terminal Degree:
96%

Student-to-Faculty Ratio:
9:1

Average Course Load:
4

Graduation Rates:
Four-Year: 81%
Five-Year: 87%
Six-Year: 90%

Special Degree Options

None

AP Test Score Requirements

Scores of four or five make one eligible for credit except in chemistry, in which a five is required. No credit is bestowed for statistics, physics B, environmental studies, international English language, and world history.

Art – One credit

Biology – One credit

Chemistry – One credit after successfully passing CHEM51.

Computer Science – One credit each for A and AB; credit removed if you take CSCI 50

Economics – One credit if both Micro and Macro exams are taken, credit removed if both ECON51 and ECON52 are passed.

English – One credit

French (language or literature, not both) – One credit, removed if student takes FREN33.

German Language – One credit, removed if GERM33 passed.

Government and Politics – One credit

History (US and European) – One credit each

Latin – One credit

Math – One course credit is given for a score of 4 or 5 on the Calculus AB or the Calculus BC. "AB Subscore" when Calculus II (Math 31) or its equivalent has been taken and passed with a grade of C- or better. Two course credits are given for Calculus BC when Calculus III (Math 32) or its equivalent has been taken and passed with a grade of C- or better.

Music Theory – One credit

Physics – No credit is given for the Physics B exam. One-half course credit is given for a score of 4 or 5 on the Physics C: Mechanics exam upon completion of Physics 51A or 51H. One-half course credit is given for a score of 4 or 5 on the Physics C: Electricity and Magnetism exam upon completion of Physics 51B.

Psychology – One credit, removed if PSYC51 passed.

Spanish – One credit, removed if SPAN33 completed.

Best Places to Study

Honnold Library, Smith Campus Center, the Quad

Sample Academic Clubs

Association for Women in Science, Economics Club, Mathematics Club

Did You Know?

Pomona College **offers the lovely and often-used P/NC option, which is short for Pass/No Credit**. If previous to the P/NC deadline, which generally falls a month or so into the semester, it becomes evident to you that you are in big trouble in, say, Advanced Calculus, just P/NC it. As long as the class wasn't for your major, if you fail it, there is no permanent mark on your transcript. If you pass it, then you get the credit, and it doesn't affect your GPA.

Acclaimed novelist **David Foster Wallace** (*Infinite Jest, Brief Interviews with Hideous Men*) joined the Pomona College faculty in the fall of 2002 as a full-time creative writing professor. The position was created with a grant from Roy E. Disney (son of Walt Disney) specifically designed to land Pomona a distinguished author on the faculty.

The average Pomona student's **GPA hovers around the B+/ A- range**. This is due to either exceptional students or grade inflation? You make the call.

Students Speak Out On...
Academics

> "I haven't had one bad professor; they're all so enthusiastic about the material it's hard not to be interested."

Q "**The teachers, for the most part, are fabulous**. They definitely want to help their students and are readily available outside of the classroom. I developed several close connections with my professors and am very grateful for their intelligence, enthusiasm, and patience."

Q "In general, the teachers are excellent. **Many of my teachers have been passionate and knowledgeable** about their subject and their students. I have bounced around from major to major over the course of my stay at Pomona and have found most classes engaging, whether it was in the English, economics, politics, or geology department. Classes are small, which really enables students to engage with both the subject matter and their professors on a more intimate level."

Q "The teachers generally **care about your well-being**. Some are amazing, and some are clinically insane. Classes are usually unfocused enough that you can make them as interesting as you want to."

Q "The professors at Pomona are, for the most part, amazing. Some of them will become your friends. Some of them will become your idols. Is there any point in going to a school where this is not possible? I don't think so. **My classes were interesting** when I chose to take challenging classes. Some classes are pretty dull, but one can avoid those."

Q "Obviously, the Pomona barrel contained some bad apples, but **even my average experience was good**, and I had some outstanding and very supportive teachers."

Q "Certain **professors are real opinion-polarizers**. Ideally, you should survey the widest cross-section of upperclassmen you can before you register for anything. People are more than happy to endorse their favorites and to warn you off the occasional nut-job. I relied pretty heavily on the add-drop period, but it didn't always work out. Bad classes are fun to complain about for a while, but by the middle of the semester, they're just demoralizing. As far as I know, there are no good statistics classes."

Q "The teachers were smart, but **apathetic about pushing students academically**."

Q "My teachers, **in the humanities at least, were altogether pathetic**. They inspired a level of mediocrity in their students which I have not encountered before or since. I think they accomplished this by not really expecting anything in the way of hard work or independent thought from their students, and then by giving more than half of them As anyway."

Q "There are lots of great professors, and **there are some that aren't so great**. It all depends on what classes you take, and who you take for those classes. My ID 1, Marriage, Motherhood, and Money, was really interesting, but I didn't expect my Calculus 3 class, for instance, to be that interesting, since it's kind of a dry subject."

Q "There are definitely good teachers here, but **you have to seek them out**. I generally ask upperclassmen or people who have had the professor already before taking a class. On the whole, I have had more good profs than bad, and there are certainly some outstanding ones, but there are some less desirable ones, as well. You just have to be discerning."

Q "Most of the faculty are **leaders in their fields**. They are extremely successful in their own research, but more importantly, they have a genuine love of undergraduate teaching. Classes are small with lots of personal interaction and engaging discussion. Professors are easily accessible to students seeking help."

Q "Some professors are brilliant, but **they take hunting around to find sometimes**. Talk to people about who to check out and who to avoid. I am now taking a class with the professor who's now my advisor and academic hero because an upperclassman friend recommended him."

Q "The teachers are **enthusiastic and helpful**. They are always accessible and are genuinely interested in making sure you understand. They do work hard to make the classes interesting; even classes I didn't like and had to take for some requirement engaged me at some point because of the work the teachers put in."

The College Prowler Take On...
Academics

Classes at Pomona aren't just small, they're intimate. If you are afraid of intimacy, be warned; you will be expected to participate at Pomona. You won't be listening to tape-recorded lectures in a hall full of 500 disinterested students. Classes are largely discussion based, and if you don't keep up, you won't just be threatened with grade penalization, your peers might think less of you, as well! Remember, academic discussion is like a multi-fronted battle, and you must defend your position, crushing your opposition until you stand alone and victorious over the smoking remains of your foe's slaughtered, rhetorical remains! Actually, discussion classes at Pomona are more like a friendly meeting than a battle. Students and professors tend to be very accepting of diverse and diverting ideas (occasionally even to a fault). As for professors, they are accessible, interesting, and generally at least as engaged in their teaching duties as they are in trying to get their latest academic treatises published. They are wonderful resources and guides when a student is self-motivated, but tend to do little to inspire the chronically apathetic—many say that Pomona makes it too easy for the lazy to slide by. Overall, what you'll find at Pomona is a bunch of professors with varied expectations for their students; some are easy graders, some are not; some will push you, and some will do everything in their power to make sure you don't have to work a lick.

Then again, when you stay up drinking every night, skip half of the assignments, and still pull down a solid B+/A- in every class, something might be a little fishy.

The College Prowler® Grade on
Academics: A-

A high Academics grade generally indicates that professors are knowledgeable, accessible, and genuinely interested in their students' welfare. Other determining factors include class size, how well professors communicate, and whether or not classes are engaging.

Local Atmosphere

The Lowdown On...
Local Atmosphere

Region:
West

City, State:
Claremont, California

Setting:
Small city

**Distance from
Los Angeles:**
45 minutes

**Distance from
San Diego:**
2 hours

Points of Interest:
Bernard Field Station

Foothills Wilderness Park

The big partially-finished marble statue in the small park in the center of Claremont (No, there really isn't anything more interesting than that in the Village)

➔

Closest Shopping Malls:

Montclair Plaza
9738 Central Ave.
Montclair, CA 91763
(909) 626-2715

Ontario Mills Shopping
Center
1 Mills Cir.
Ontario, CA 91764
(909) 484-8301
www.ontariomills.com

Students in the know claim
that the best shopping
outside of Los Angeles
can be found in downtown
Pasadena.

Closest Movie Theaters:

AMC in Covina
1414 N. Azusa Ave.
Covina, CA 91722
(626) 974-8600

Ontario Mills
4549 Mills Cir.
Ontario, CA 91764
(909) 484-3000

Major Sports Teams:

Anaheim Angels at
Los Angeles (baseball)

Los Angeles Clippers
(basketball)

Los Angeles Dodgers
(baseball)

Los Angeles Lakers
(basketball)

City Web Sites

www.ci.claremont.ca.us

Did You Know?

5 Fun Facts about Claremont:

- Claremont's **median income is $66,547**, much of which, judging by the average age of the inhabitants, must consist of retirement pensions.

- Acclaimed pop-artist **Ben Harper's extended family runs an acoustic music store** in the Village, and every now and then, Ben will drop in and "kick it."

- Tired of the kitschy Claremont atmosphere? Just enter the festively-muraled alleyway beside Heroes Bar and you'll find **Nick's Café, the closest thing Claremont has to subculture**. It's frequented by Celtic-Goth kids, mostly the jobless, 20-something, estranged children of wealthy Claremont residents.

- Claremont is far from a bastion of public art, but you can find a marble statue in the center of town that resembles **a caveman playing a lyre**, while some more modern fellow looks over his shoulder and a kid and a cat climb in a tree. There are many childrens' handprints on the back of the statue. The statue was sculpted, on site, a few years back, and the process was one of the major attractions in Claremont for a while.

- Famed rapper **Snoop Dogg lives in northern Claremont**, and although you may not like his music, he is a solid member of the community. Last year, he volunteer-coached a local sports team.

Famous People from Claremont/Inland Empire:

Sammy Hagar	Tim Robbins
Ben Harper	Snoop Dogg
Tommy Lee	Forest Whitaker
Steve McQueen	Robin Williams
Demi Moore	

→

Local Slang:

"Fo' Shizzle!" – Actually a variant of "For Sheezy," which means "for sure," as in "I'm going to ace that test fo' shizzle!" Remember, Snoop makes his home in Claremont. (He, at least as far as pop culture is concerned, is the progenitor of this particular phrase, and the entire trend of taking the first consonant of a word, dropping the rest, and adding "-izzle." Try it, and amaze your friends and families alike. E.g., Hey mo-fizzle! Get on up off my shizzle before I kizzle your izzle!)

"Bra," as in "what's kickin', Bra" – No, not an over-the-shoulder boulder-holder, but rather a SoCal version of "bro," which is, of course, a popular truncation of "brother."

Students Speak Out On...
Local Atmosphere

"The atmosphere is very hazy. Sometimes it smells bad, but generally, it smells okay. Stay on campus. Do not visit anything."

Q "The campus is beautiful, but the **surrounding area leaves much to be desired**. A car is very helpful."

Q "The town is quiet, and generally, it is an entirely separate community from the colleges. There are stores, restaurants, banks, and other services that college students use gladly and often, but they're not specifically catered to the students. Visiting the other four Claremont Colleges adds a lot of variety to life and helps us meet new people. **A lot of people take trips into LA on the Metrolink train**, which has a station right in town. For about eight dollars round trip you can get to Union Station in LA, and from there take the light-rail line on your Metrolink ticket to places like Long Beach, Hollywood, and Redondo Beach. People also drive to the usual attractions like movies, the mall, and Disneyland. The ASPC office has discounted movie and theme-park tickets. We also have easy access to both skiing and beaches."

Q "**The town sucks**! Most of it isn't geared to college students, despite the fact that we have a significant presence in the town. There's nothing to do at all. You need a car to seek any kind of off-campus entertainment."

Q "The atmosphere is **sunny and sleepy in Claremont**. It's an upper-class retirement community. Thank goodness we have the other Claremont Colleges with which to socialize. It's fun to go to Bert and Rocky's ice cream place, and to browse the tiny shops in Claremont, but everything is too expensive to buy."

Q "Claremont is **a little boring**, but beautiful and a great place to spend four years."

Q "I don't spend much time in Claremont; **it's mostly just expensive antique stores and mediocre restaurants**. The close proximity of the other four colleges makes Pomona feel like a much larger school, which is good sometimes. You can always go eat at another school's dining hall for a change of pace. Also, having the other colleges adds to the social life."

Q "Even though there are five colleges in Claremont, **it's not a college town**. Students can't really afford anything there. I think Claremont Village is run by the Mafia, since all the stores are clearly covers for illicit activities. However, the farmer's market on Sunday mornings is really nice and wonderful. I don't think the farmer's market has anything to do with the Mafia."

Q "The atmosphere in Claremont is that of a small town full of college students. However, the **students do not rule the town**; they rule only the campuses. Get out of Claremont and spend some time in Los Angeles—whole weekends, if possible. It is beautiful, and there is so much to do there. So take a car to school if you can, and leave the Inland Empire. Or take your car to the desert, or the mountains, which are both close to Claremont."

Q "There are five colleges surrounding Claremont. The **town is fun if you like eating pastry and drinking coffee all day** (which I did), but not very much fun if you're looking for a big city, or even kind of a big-city atmosphere. Stay away from spending all your money on coffee just because you get bored in Claremont because there's nothing else to do."

Q "Claremont is a **retirement community**, and there is a constant battle between the students and permanent residents. It's fun."

Q "Claremont? It's pleasant, quaint. Outside of Claremont is **similar to New Jersey**."

Q "Now that you are living in Claremont, this will be a good time to **expand your porcelain kitten collection**."

Q "The other four colleges of the Claremont Consortium are all within walking distance and drastically expand the social horizons of what would otherwise be an exceptionally small social group. The town of Claremont that immediately surrounds the colleges **does not have much to offer students** other than a few good places to eat. Fortunately, the college is near the mountains and a network of hiking/mountain-biking trails that provide plenty of opportunities for recreation if you like those types of activities. Also, the colleges are close enough to LA if that is more your style, as long as you don't mind fighting the infamous Inland Empire traffic."

Q "**People should visit LA**. (Like anyone's going to go to Pomona and not go to LA.) They should go to the La Brea tar pits. They should go to the Norton Simon in Pasadena which is more interesting and 'do-able' than LACMA. They should go to the Getty when, and only when, the garden is in bloom. They should see Venice Beach. They should just drive around through LA and ponder its weirdness. They should also go to Joshua Tree and hike, rock climb, get dehydrated, and call it a spiritual experience or whatever."

The College Prowler Take On...
Local Atmosphere

Well, now you've heard it from the horses' mouths, and contrary to aphorism, feel free to look in these horses' mouths, and even to count their teeth, because they're not selling you a load of bull. Claremont just isn't cut out to be a college town. There isn't anything to do except walk around and buy overpriced doo-dads, which (i.e., the doo-dads) your grandmother might find appealing (not to cast aspersions on your grandmother's taste), but which (i.e., the doo-dads again) will likely leave you unimpressed. LA is great, but only if you have a car. Public transit to LA just doesn't cut it for evening excursions. The Inland Empire (the area surrounding Claremont) is pretty trashy, and except for a few dive bars, doesn't have much to offer in the way of activities. Oh yeah. There is a flea market in the Inland Empire, but why anyone would want to buy fleas is beyond me ...

Claremont is far more of a retirement community than it is a college town; you will exhaust its entertainment potential in about a day. Los Angeles is a cultural mecca (well, at least a cultural hub) and boasts tons of museums (if you can, check out the Museum of Jurassic Technology), stores, beaches, clubs, and bars, and you'll have a difficult time running out of things to do there. The other colleges provide a nice break from Pomona, but aren't, when you get right down to it, really different enough from Pomona to constitute an off-campus experience. Prepare to be absorbed by the giant social black hole that is Pomona College.

The College Prowler® Grade on

Local Atmosphere: C-

A high Local Atmosphere grade indicates that the area surrounding campus is safe and scenic. Other factors include nearby attractions, proximity to other schools, and the town's attitude toward students.

Safety & Security

The Lowdown On...
Safety & Security

**Number of
Pomona Police:**

22 full-time, 28 part-time

Pomona Police Phone:

(909) 607-2000

Safety Services:

Student Escort Service
(available every night from
7 p.m.–1 a.m.) Provides rides
(on richly-appointed golf carts)
to students who do not wish to
walk home alone. The number
is (909) 607-2101.

Health Services

Urgent care, cold/flu care, free appointments, screening, STD testing, confidential HIV testing, mono testing, strep testing, EKG, pulmonary testing, peak flow, medications (prescriptions and over the counter), physical exams, X-ray and lab services, minor surgery (suturing, wart removal), medical supplies, dermatology, immunizations, women's health (annual exam including pap smear, contraception, and counseling), urinary tract infection treatment.

Health Center Office Hours

Monday–Friday (excluding Wednesday) 8:30 a.m.–5 p.m.
(909) 621-8222

Did You Know?

An appointment at Pomona's Baxter Building is free (medication and procedures are billed to your student account), but a walk-in costs 10 dollars.

Students Speak Out On...
Safety & Security

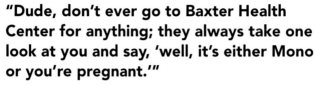

"Dude, don't ever go to Baxter Health Center for anything; they always take one look at you and say, 'well, it's either Mono or you're pregnant.'"

Q "**Security is very good**. Security guys zip around on golf carts all the time. There are lighted security stations with phones all over campus. RAs are always on call and are easy to get a hold of. I feel very safe walking across campus in the middle of the night."

Q "I always feel **very safe**, even when it's late and I'm by myself. Once, at 4:30 a.m. on a rare foggy night, when I had to go all the way across campus by myself, I called Campus Security for an escort."

Q "I've never had any problems. **Stuff gets stolen sometimes**, but thievery isn't rampant."

Q "It's fine. **I never felt unsafe**, and I would frequently walk around at night alone. Naked."

Q "I feel pretty secure and safe, but **I lock my door when I leave my room** for a long time, and I think it's nice that we have escort services, locks on the outside doors, and lighted walkways. I think I'd still walk home with a friend from a party at 2 a.m., though."

Q "**You don't have to worry about security** and safety messing with the fun, crazy, reckless life on campus. Unless you make the wrong students mad, in which case things will be made really bad for you, or so I hear."

Q "Seriously, **it is like being back in the womb or something**. You may get your bike stolen, but I never ran into any dangerous people. Most crimes on Pomona's campus are acts of petty vandalism committed by Pomona students who are generally given a slap on the wrist."

Q "The campus feels very safe. Because Pomona is a smaller school, **there is a greater sense of community** in which people generally look out for each other. However, as on any college campus, the consumption of alcohol increases both the vulnerability of victims and the likelihood of predatory sexual behavior."

Q "It feels safe, although **I rarely encounter security guards**."

Q "As far as physical safety, **it's perfectly fine unless you're a sheltered suburban kid** who can't deal with a couple of lost, stammering homeless dudes who get escorted off campus by security after being there for less than a minute. There is a lot of computer theft, though."

Q "Campus is safe. Probably **too safe**."

Q "Security seems fine on campus. **I never really felt in danger** or anything like that, but the campus is often times pretty desolate because of the small student body."

Q "Security seems **adequate**. The security guards are all very friendly."

The College Prowler Take On...
Safety & Security

Pomona security officers are generally laid-back, eager to help, and loathe to make your, and thus their, lives more difficult. They are far more likely to warn you than cite you for most minor infractions. Most of them want to be your friend, and it's hard to be friends with someone who's all up in your bidness! One particularly gregarious guard even used to lead rap freestyles at parties.

Pomona is a safe campus; there are hardly ever any incidents (except for bike theft—no one knows who steals all the bikes, but whoever it is must have a garage the size of an airplane hangar to hold all the spare parts they've accumulated), and when there are incidents, the security officers usually respond promptly and professionally. Sometimes, the administration does get a little too concerned with currying student favor to perform their duties to the fullest. Student escorts are available for those who don't wish to travel the campus alone at night, and cab rides home from the surrounding area for drunk students are free with a college ID.

The College Prowler® Grade on

Safety & Security: A

A high grade in Safety & Security means that students generally feel safe, campus police are visible, blue-light phones and escort services are readily available, and safety precautions are not overly necessary.

Computers

The Lowdown On...
Computers

High-Speed Network?
Yes

Wireless Network?
Yes

Number of Labs:
12

Operating Systems:
Windows XP, Mac OSX, Linux

Numbers of Computers:
900

Free Software

Windows OS software and Microsoft Office are available to all students and staff for use on their personal machines—contact Information & Technology Services at (909) 621-8061.

24-Hour Labs

Two labs

Charge to Print?

Five cents per page

Did You Know?

If you have any need to send an all-campus e-mail, it's as easy as the push of a button. However, **the service is occasionally abused**. In spring of '05, the student body President (who, here, shall remain nameless, but who was, for the record, the brains behind the 2005 senior class slogan "'05 is OK,") sent an all-student e-mail announcing that the administration had decided, with a month left in the semester, to institute mandatory drug-testing as a requisite for graduation. This e-mail, sent on April 1st, (oh what fools we were), sparked a near-Orwellian panic in Pomona's population before a few somewhat-more-savvy-than-the-rest-of-us students pointed out that it was April Fools Day. These sort of pranks are met with a hearty "ha ha" from administration and student alike, but any mean-spirited abuse of the all-student's e-mail is met with strict penalties, such as revocation of one's Internet privileges, a fate only marginally worse than death.

Students Speak Out On...
Computers

"We have a school network with T1 Internet access and campus-wide file-sharing capabilities. It's generally very good, and we have an ITS staff to help with some computer issues."

Q "There are **quite a few computer labs on campus**, with modern equipment and software, which are never very crowded. I would recommend bringing your own computer, but if absolutely necessary, there are always school computers to use. There is even network space allotted to each student so they can save work and files anywhere on campus."

Q "Internet is **easy and fast**; wireless Internet is getting much better—cutting edge."

Q "Definitely **bring a computer of your own**; you'll use it a lot. Most classes require some Internet access, even if it's just for e-mailing the professor, and it's much more convenient to have your own computer. I use the computer labs for printing and scanning. They generally are not too crowded. The network itself often leaves something to be desired. It goes down fairly often, and I got a computer virus from it once."

Q "I have my own computer, but if for some reason I use a computer lab, **it always works nicely**, and I never have had a problem finding a computer available."

Q "The computer labs are **never crowded**, because everyone has a computer. I would and did bring one, because the homework is so heavy that I wouldn't want to be stuck in a lab for that long. We do have lots of Macs and PCs on campus, although Macs aren't dominant in the student population, and don't work well for file-share. I still have mine, though, and there are authorities who can help on Mac 'issues.'"

Q "The computer **labs are great** and one can almost always find a place to work, but it is nice to have your own computer if you want to look at some of the more extreme Web sites out there."

Q "**I don't use the labs**; almost everyone has their own computer at Pomona."

Q "The network is **good depending on which dorm you live in** (some have newer/faster wiring), although it does crash upon occasion. There is generally space in the computer labs, but due to the volume of work assigned, it is essential to have a computer available in your own room."

Q "Bring your own computer. **When else will your parents buy you a computer**? If you can't bring your own computer, you'll be fine. You'll just sort of live in the computer lab."

Q "It's up to you. There are **lots of computer labs open 24 hours** if you want, but it's always nice to have your own machine."

Q "The campus network is **very fragile and very sensitive**, and when people start stressing out, it tends to shut down. You're definitely going to want your own printer."

Q "Having your own computer is worthwhile. The computer facilities are good but **can get too crowded during finals**."

The College Prowler Take On...
Computers

Pomona students, although a fun-loving, laid-back bunch, do have a lot of homework, and much of this is performed on futuristic machines called "computers." If you've never seen one, they are sort of like televisions, except, get this, interactive! The general consensus on the campus' technical options is that the computer situation is so-so. There are certainly more-wired and better-run campuses as per computers, but if you are an atavist who just longs for the heady thwack of the typewriter keys impacting crisp, white paper, then you aren't going to find it here (unless you create your own heady thwacks). There are two 24-hour computer labs in which you will almost always be able to find a computer (there are times when you can't, however) and plenty of Pomona students/com-geeks are at your beck and call to troubleshoot all your computer problems. They even make house calls! They are like the plumbers of the information age!

The Pomona network is sizable and heavily trafficked, and many classes require accessing online databases and discussion groups. This said, it is certainly possible to get by without being some sort of computer wiz—there are plenty of nerds available to lend a helping hand. Of course, no hands (no matter how ink stained and pallid) can help when the network goes down, as often happens, right before you need to print and turn in a paper. It's a good idea to get your work done ahead of time, because professors tend to have low tolerance for tech-related excuses. This is probably because most of them still live in the stone age; many of them still subscribe to ideologies that require them to write everything by hand!

B

The College Prowler® Grade on

Computers: B

A high grade in Computers designates that computer labs are available, the computer network is easily accessible, and the campus' computing technology is up-to-date.

Facilities

The Lowdown On...
Facilities

Athletic Center:
The Rains Center

Student Center:
Smith Campus Center

Library:
Honnold Mudd Library

Campus Size:
140 acres

Popular Places to Chill:
Campus Center courtyard
The Motley (at Scripps)
Marston Quad
The pool

What Is There to Do on Campus?

Go to a movie on Friday, Saturday, or Sunday in the Rose Hills Theater. It costs two dollars, but if you are willing to skip the first five-minutes of the movie, which generally consist of previews, you can walk in for free.

Hit the state-of-the-art weights in the Rains Center, but not when the football players are in there because it is demoralizing, embarrassing, and sometimes scary for those who are less hypertrophic.

Take a dip in either the recreational or official Olympic pool (during hours or after—breaking into the South Campus pool is one of Pomona's finest traditions. Students who are caught are merely escorted from the premises and you are allowed some time to re-robe, if necessary).

Movie Theater on Campus?

Yes, the Rose Hills Theater in the Campus Center.

Bowling on Campus?

No

Bar on Campus?

No

Coffeehouse on Campus?

No

Favorite Things to Do

Pomona's weekend movies are always well attended, as are the college plays, of which there are many. Many students tout the merits of a hard workout at Rains followed by a bout of sauna-sitting, but if this is your activity of choice, remember to keep hydrated. There are also frequent, and frequently well attended, lectures and concerts in the Campus Center.

Students Speak Out On...
Facilities

> "Facilities on campus are beautiful and incredible. Everything is nice and never crowded."

"Everything is very nice. **The school renovates all the time**. Smith Campus Center is only a few years old and has lots of good facilities and resources for students, like the Career Development Office, Student Government Office, study lounges, two restaurants, a store, an ATM, the mail room, and even a small movie theater in the basement."

"All facilities are **state-of-the-art** and well maintained."

"All of the facilities are really nice and are very **impressive for such a small school**. Most of the stuff in the Rains Center is almost brand new, like the weight machines and stuff. The pool is really nice too."

"I don't know what their dumb excuse is for closing the weight room as early as they do, but **it's bullcrap**."

"Well, I'm not that into athletics, but **everything looks well-kept-up**, and I've heard that we have an awesome couple of indoor basketball courts. The computer lab is very up-to-date with a ton of available help. The student center is fabulous, and Frary Dining Hall is really beautiful, but a little loud for intimate conversation."

"**The gym really sucks**. I used the Tulane gym all summer, and it has so many windows, new machines, wide treadmills, and other nice things. Not at Pomona. The Campus Center is charmless and creepy. "

Q "I have a friend who used to refer to the Smith Campus Center as 'the Fascist Sublime.' It is cozier than it used to be, I guess, especially now that they've gotten rid of all those cheap plastic chairs in the Coop, but it still seems to be designed more for trustees than for students. **The mail room is only slightly larger than my bathroom**. And why can't we use the nice rooms? All the nice rooms are always locked."

Q "Nice facilities; **everything's up-to-date**."

Q "The **facilities are excellent** at Pomona."

Q "Our facilities are **wonderful**, of course—only the best."

Q "**Athletic facilities suck**. Most likely your high school facilities were better. The Campus Center is, I believe, aesthetically nice, but lots of kids don't like it much."

The College Prowler Take On...
Facilities

Pomona students have mixed opinions on their college facilities. This could either be because the facilities are highly controversial, or it could be because, as liberal arts students, they are trained to always explore opposing viewpoints. The Campus Center, Rains Center, and library are all large and impressive, especially considering the size of the college, but many find them unappealing, unpragmatically designed, and even garish. Others, of course, rave about them, but it is a fact that the facilities generally seem designed more to impress than to, well, facilitate the activities that they were designed to facilitate.

You won't ever feel crowded in Pomona's facilities (except for the cursed mail room—you won't ever not feel crowded in the cursed mail room), which is a definite plus. There are only 1400 students and the facilities rival many larger schools for sheer size. Pomona facilities tend to follow the recipe of form over function, but the form mainly follows an aesthetic of "bigger is better."

B+

The College Prowler® Grade on
Facilities: B+

A high Facilities grade indicates that the campus is aesthetically pleasing and well-maintained; facilities are state-of-the-art, and libraries are exceptional. Other determining factors include the quality of both athletic and student centers and an abundance of things to do on campus.

Campus Dining

The Lowdown On...
Campus Dining

Freshman Meal Plan Requirement?
Yes

Meal Plan Average Cost:
Roughly $3,000

(There is a certain amount of flexibility due to different meal plans with varying amounts of flex-dollars).

Places to Grab a Bite with Your Meal Plan:

The Coop Fountain
Food: Fast food
Location: The Campus Center
Hours: Monday–Thursday
9 a.m.–12 a.m.,
Friday 9 a.m.–1:30 a.m.,
Saturday 12 p.m.–1:30 a.m.,
Sunday 12 p.m.–12 a.m.

Frank Dining Hall

Food: Varied, vegetarian options

Location: South Campus

Hours: Monday–Friday 7:30 a.m.–10 a.m., 11:30 a.m.–1 p.m., 5 p.m.–7 p.m., Saturday–Sunday 11 a.m.–1 p.m., 5:30 p.m.–7:30 p.m.

Frary Dining Hall

Food: Varied, vegetarian options

Location: North Campus

Hours: Monday–Friday 7:30 a.m.–10 a.m., 11:30 a.m.–1 a.m., 5 p.m.–8 p.m., Saturday–Sunday 9 a.m.–1 p.m., 5:30 p.m.–7 p.m.

Oldenborg

Food: International

Location: Mid-Campus

Hours: Monday–Friday 7:30 a.m.–10 a.m., 11:30 a.m.–1 a.m., 5 p.m.–8 p.m., Saturday–Sunday 9 a.m.–1 p.m., 5:30 p.m.–7 p.m.

Sagehen Café

Food: Pasta, salads, wraps

Location: Campus Center

Hours: Monday–Wednesday 11 a.m.–2 p.m., Thursday–Friday 11 a.m.–2 p.m., 5 p.m.–9 p.m., Saturday 5 p.m.–9 p.m.

Off-Campus Places to Use Your Meal Plan:

None

24-Hour On-Campus Eating?

No

Other Options:

Eating at other campuses—Collins (the CMC dining hall) and Mallot Commons (the Scripps dining hall) are particular favorites.

Student Favorites:

The Coop Fountain

Did You Know?

Pomona's Frary Dining Hall is graced with **a giant mural by Jose Orozco of Prometheus**. The giant, fire-bringing half-god is pictured writhing amidst all sorts of dark and portentous figures, one of whom resembles a fetal fawn with a baby's head—just what students want to see when they're eating. In the '50s, when it was painted, the college officials were worried about female students seeing ol' Prometheus's package, and so they had it painted over. To this day, Prometheus, without whom none of us would have fire, remains emasculated.

Many students tout the merits of **sneaking into Frank Dining Hall**, which merely requires scaling a five-foot wall out back. Yes, it's easy (except when the back door is being guarded), but remember that crime doesn't pay. Unless you are really, really hungry and have no other options for obtaining sustenance. In that case, a good argument could be made for it paying.

It's also possible to sneak into Frary Dining Hall during off hours, but it requires **scaling buildings and shimmying through ducts**, and when you finally get in, all the food is locked away anyway.

Students Speak Out On...
Campus Dining

> **"The food on campus is the best at the dining halls of other colleges, especially the butternut squash soup at Scripps."**

Q "The food is good. **The quality is about standard**, but there is a lot of selection. The school pays special attention to special-needs eaters like vegetarians and vegans and gives them a lot of special options, as well. To add more variety to the routine, we can eat at any of the dining halls on any of the five campuses. Frary was just renovated and now, along with the usual dining hall-fare, has a pizza oven and a choose-your-own-ingredients stir-fry wok at every meal."

Q "Food **on campus is delicious** and nicer than the food at many restaurants."

Q "The food is actually **really good**. Both dining halls were recently remodeled. They try really hard to keep a variety of food in the dining halls, which some places don't even bother doing. There's lots of made-to-order stuff, and the food tends to be good quality. The Coop Fountain has really good food, too, if you want to take a break from dining hall food."

Q "By the time you're a junior, you know that **the food on campus sucks**. The best available food is actually at Claremont McKenna. Their sandwich meats are of noticeably higher quality, and they have three different kinds of mustard. Scripps is second best. Their oven-fresh cookies are hard to beat. Arguably, Scrippsies are less annoying to look at than CMCers while you're eating."

Q "**Food on campus is okay**. Scripps has better food."

Q "The food is **pretty good**. I would say it is excellent for me, but some people complain that it gets boring. If it does get repetitious, then you can go to the Coop and get shakes, smoothies, burgers, and quesadillas."

Q "It is easy to sneak into Frank Dining Hall by hopping over one five-foot wall and then going in the back door; **I would recommend this in a pinch**, though the food is not that good. With a little planning, you can easily sneak into more desirable dining halls (CMC and Mallot Commons being my favorites) by learning which entrances are unguarded at which times."

Q "The food on campus is **pretty exceptional** relative to most college food. Each dining hall generally offers three to four entrées for each meal, which include vegetarian and vegan options, as well as an excellent salad bar and sandwich bar at lunch."

Q "Students at the Claremont Colleges can use their meal plan to eat at any of the dining halls at the 5Cs, so **there is excellent variety** within a short walk. In addition to the dining halls, there are several on-campus restaurants, which serve everything from quesadillas and burgers to fresh seafood pasta."

Q "The dining halls rock, but **spoiled, bratty students love to gripe about the food**. In Frary, you're dining in about as much style as you'll ever see on a college campus."

Q "The dining hall is alright. **There are lots more vegetarian and vegan options** than there are at other schools. With the newly renovated Frary Dining Hall, there is great potential for even better fare."

Q "I was **pleased with the food on campus**. The salad bar is always stocked full of fresh and glorious vegetables and fruit."

Q "Sausage pizza soup: **how did they even make that**?"

Q "The food at Pomona is **not terrible**, but it's nothing to rave about."

The College Prowler Take On...
Campus Dining

The quality of campus food service is a common target for complaint and ridicule among students, but Pomona actually does a pretty good job. No, it's not gourmet, nor probably even commensurate with your dear mother's cooking, but Pomona's dining halls offer a large variety of dining options. Students particularly laud the design-your-own meals, which range from pizza to stir-fry and have become more and more of a fixture in recent years. The option of attending the other colleges' dining halls also provides some needed variety. The dining hall staff also goes to great lengths, unfortunately with very mixed results, to meet the needs of those with dietary restrictions.

Pomona dining inspires mixed reviews. There are a staggering amount of options, but you get a nagging feeling that the food just isn't that fresh. However, preparing meals, day in and day out, for 1,400 hungry students with a whole slew of dietary preferences and restrictions must be a staggering task. There is a good dynamic between Frary and Frank dining halls, the former being an enormous, cathedral-esque hall, the latter being far more modern and varied in design. Vegetarians and vegans certainly won't starve, though they may end up eating a lot of plain pasta and bagels, and nightly "Snack," which is a sort of ad-hoc meal each weeknight from 10:30 p.m. to midnight, not only provides late-night sustenance, but serves as a sort of social event, as well. One thing you can definitely say for the dining hall staff is that they try very hard to mix things up. However, they are consistently inconsistent, which can at times be very frustrating for an on-campus diner.

B+

The College Prowler® Grade on

Campus Dining: B+

Our grade on Campus Dining addresses the quality of both school-owned dining halls and independent on-campus restaurants as well as the price, availability, and variety of food.

Off-Campus Dining

The Lowdown On...
Off-Campus Dining

Restaurant Prowler:
Popular Places to Eat!

42nd Street Bagel
Food: Bagels
225 Yale Ave.
(909) 624-7655
Cool Features: The entire thing is decorated with Broadway musical paraphernalia.
Price: $2–$6 per person
Hours: Monday–Friday 6 a.m.–6 p.m., Saturday–Sunday 7 a.m.–5 p.m.

Aruffos
Food: Italian
126 Yale Ave.
(909) 624-9624
Cool Features: Noodles, lots and lots of noodles
Price: $8–14 per person
Hours: Sunday–Thursday 11 a.m.–8:30 p.m., Friday–Saturday 11 a.m.–9:30 p.m.

Del Taco
Food: Mexican
1653 W Foothill Blvd.
(909) 920-3464

➜

(Del Taco, continued)

Cool Features: Great for late-night dining and drive-thru.

Price: $6–$12 per person

Hours: Daily 24 hours

Delhi Palace Express

Food: Indian fast food

313 Yale Ave.

(909) 626-6030

Cool Features: All day, all-you-can-eat buffet.

Price: $7–$13 per person

Hours: Daily 11 a.m.–9 p.m.

Domino's Pizza

Food: Pizza

366 W Foothill Blvd.

(909) 398-0404

Price: $6–$15 per person

Hours: Sunday–Thursday 10 a.m.–12 a.m., Friday–Saturday 10 a.m.–1 a.m.

Full of Life

Food: Bakery, sandwiches

333 W Bonita Ave.

(909) 624-3420

Cool Features: All sanwiches come on crusty, freshly-baked breads.

Price: $6–$9 per person

Hours: Sunday–Monday 8 a.m.–3 p.m., Tuesday–Saturday 8 a.m.–5 p.m.

Harvard Square Café

Food: French

206 W Bonita Ave.

(909) 626-7763

(Harvard Square, continued)

Cool Features: Three entirely separate dining areas, each themed differently.

Price: $11–$20 per person

Hours: Sunday–Thurday 11 a.m.–9 p.m., Friday–Saturday 11 a.m.–10 p.m.

The Hat

Food: Fried food, burgers

857 N Central Ave.

(909) 949-4607

Cool Features: The famous, thinly-sliced pastrami dip sandwich.

Price: $4–$8 per person

Hours: Monday–Saturday 9 a.m.–1 a.m., Sunday 10 a.m.–1 a.m.

In-N-Out Burger

Food: Fast food

2098 Foothill Blvd.

(800) 786-1000

Price: $3–$7 per person

Hours: Daily 24 hours

Mix Bowl Café

Food: Thai

1520 Indian Hill Blvd.

(909) 447-4401

Cool Features: Late-night on-campus delivery.

Price: $5–$10 per person

Hours: Daily 11 a.m.–2 a.m.

Pizza 'N Such

Food: Pizza, sandwiches

273 W 2nd St.

(909) 624-7214

(Pizza 'N Such, continued)

Cool Features: Sandwiches are baked in the pizza oven.

Price: $5–$10 per person

Hours: Sunday–Thursday 11 a.m.–9 p.m., Friday–Saturday 11 a.m.–10 p.m.

The Press

Food: Upscale American

129 Harvard Ave.

(909) 625-4808

Cool Features: Press Fries (a giant platter of potatoes and yuccas). And they have a bar too.

Price: $10–$15 per person

Hours: Monday 8 p.m.–12 a.m., Tuesday–Wednesday 11 a.m.–12a.m., Thursday–Saturday 11 a.m.–1 a.m., Sunday 5 p.m.–12 a.m.

Quiznos Classic Subs

Food: Submarine Sandwiches

383 W Bonita Ave.

(909) 621-9051

Price: $5–$7 per person

Hours: Monday–Saturday 10:30 a.m.–9 p.m., Sunday 11:30 a.m.–8 p.m.

Sacas Mediterranean Cuisine

Food: Mediteranean

248 W 2nd St.

(909) 624-3340

Cool Features: Huge rotating spits of meat.

Price: $7–$13 per person

Hours: Sunday–Thursday 11 a.m.–8 p.m., Friday–Saturday 11 a.m.–9 p.m.

Village Grill

Food: Vintage American

148 Yale Ave.

(909) 626-8813

Cool Features: Life sized cardboard cutout of James Dean from "Rebel Without a Cause."

Price: $5–$10 per person

Hours: Monday–Saturday 6 a.m.–8 p.m., Sunday 7 a.m.–3 p.m.

Walter's

Food: Upscale

Address: 316 Yale Ave.

(909) 624-2779

Cool Features: Ambience (if that's cool).

Price: $10–$20 per person

Hours: Monday–Saturday 7 a.m.–9 p.m., Sunday 8 a.m.–9 p.m.

Yianni's Greek Restaurant

Food: Greek

238 Yale Ave.

Phone: (909) 621-2413

Cool Features: Greek kitsch decor.

Price: $6–$12 per person

Hours: Monday–Saturday 11 a.m.–9:30 p.m., Sunday 10 a.m.–9 p.m.

Student Favorites:
Delhi Palace Express
Sacas Mediteranean Cuisine

Late-Night Delivery:
Domino's Pizza
Mix Bowl Café

Other Options:
Don José
El Pavo
Heroe's
Somecrust

24-Hour Eating:
In-N-Out,
Del Taco

Closest Grocery Store:
Wolfe's Market
160 W Foothill Blvd.
(909) 626-8508

Best Pizza:
Pizza 'N Such

Best Thai:
Mix Bowl Café

Best Breakfast:
Village Grill

Best Healthy:
Full of Life

Best Wings:
The Hat

Best Place to Take Your Parents:
Harvard Square Café
Walter's

Did You Know?

If, as is often the case in college, you are feeling a bit run down, a bit out of shape, and if, as may also often be the case, you believe that your exclusive diet of beer and nacho-cheese dip just isn't cutting it, then **hit the Village for the Sunday farmer's market**, which features organic produce and other healthy things to eat. Unfortunately, you have to wake up awfully early to get there.

Students Speak Out On...

Off-Campus Dining

"The restaurants in walking distance are mostly overpriced. Somecrust is good for sandwiches and cookies."

Q "There are **a lot of places in town**. There are traditional restaurants, like for Italian and American food, but there are also a couple of Greek places, some Mexican places, a Chinese take-out, and pizza joints. I don't go into town to eat much, but when I do, I often get a boba drink from the Chinese place and a sandwich from Full of Life bakery next door."

Q "I don't really eat off campus much. **There's a pizza place in the Village** that is pretty good called Pizza 'N Such. Also, there are good Mexican restaurants in the surrounding Pomona area."

Q "Good restaurants, but **very expensive**."

Q "Eh, the restaurants are okay, but **not worth the money**."

Q "There are several restaurants, **most beyond the average student's means**. I'm sure one exception, Delhi Palace, will get lots of press, as I believe the author of this publication is partial to it. Personally, I liked Full of Life for breakfast or a little tea-time treat. They have good variety and the seating area is usually clean and light, if a little cramped. One of their blueberry cream cheese danishes has enough calories for an entire day. This one time, I ate seven in one day. Then I didn't have to eat again for a week."

Q "Walter's is really good. It's kind of a combo of **Afghan and Italian**."

Q "The Village has **several good restaurants**, although they tend to be rather pricey. Heroe's has great burgers and beer. The New Delhi Palace has good Indian food for a reasonable price. Pizza 'N Such offers excellent pizza and relatively inexpensive beer. If you have a car, (or a friend with a car), the options are endless within the greater LA area."

Q "Burritos are **cheap and abundant**. All you have to do is go to Pomona."

Q "**Most of the restaurants within walking distance are expensive**. Save them for parent visits. Farther away, there are unlimited possibilities, including lots of authentic cheap Mexican food places."

Q "There are **not many restaurants off campus** if you don't have a car. However, local favorites include DPX (Delhi Palace Express), In-N-Out, and Del-Taco for late-night runs."

Q "For Thai food at 2 a.m., the Mix Bowl is ideal. **For cheap Mexican, El Pavo is your place**. For 48-ounce margaritas, Don José is a college student's dream."

Q "Off-campus dining is, in a word, **mediocre**. Restaurants in Claremont are way too overpriced for the crap that they serve. Try Orchid Garden on Foothill Boulevard. It's very good with exceptional service. Also, it's vegetarian-friendly."

The College Prowler Take On...
Off-Campus Dining

Students complain about the prices of most of the off-campus restaurants, but there are plenty of cheap options as well. As is always the case, you're not going to find fancy food for low prices, but in the Village you will find good food for good prices, as well as finer food for higher prices. If you are in the market for fast food, you will likely need a car, as the Village is a little too hoity-toity to have a McDonald's on the corner. The Village's deficiencies as per dining have a lot more to do with the general deficiencies of the Village as a college town than they do with the actual restaurants.

Considering the size of the Village, it is remarkably well stocked with restaurants, the one real concession to college life. However, due to the property taxes in the Village, most of the restaurants are somewhat pricey. There are exceptions though, including Delhi Palace Express, Sacas, and The Taco Factory. However, you may soon tire of these places and long for new palate-tickling dining options. When this happens, you will need a car or a friend with a car. Of course, you are more likely to be friends with someone with a car than they are likely to be friends with you. A friend in need is a friend indeed, and what, pray tell, do the automotively-privileged need that the rest of us can ever hope to provide?

The College Prowler® Grade on

Off-Campus Dining: C-

A high Off-Campus Dining grade implies that off-campus restaurants are affordable, accessible, and worth visiting. Other factors include the variety of cuisine and the availability of alternative options (vegetarian, vegan, Kosher, etc.).

Campus Housing

The Lowdown On...
Campus Housing

Room Types:
Singles, doubles,
two-room doubles

Best Dorms:
Mudd Blaisdell
Clark V

Worst Dorms:
Smiley
Wig

**Undergrads Living
on Campus:**
97%

Number of Dorms:
12

**Number of University-
Owned Apartments:**
0

Dormitories

Albert K. Smiley
Floors: 3
Total Occupancy: 60
Bathrooms: Communal
Coed: Yes
Residents: Upperclassmen
Room Types: Singles
Special Features: Lounge, laundry, smoke free

Clark I
Floors: 2
Total Occupancy: 116
Bathrooms: Shared by suite
Coed: Yes
Residents: Upperclassmen
Room Types: Primarily two-room doubles
Special Features: Courtyard access, laundry

Clark V
Floors: 2
Total Occupancy: 95
Bathroom: Shared by suite
Coed: Yes
Residents: Upperclassmen
Room Types: Some singles, some two-room doubles
Special Features: Some fireplaces in rooms, courtyard access, laundry

Cottages
Floors: 3 buildings, I floor apiece
Total Occupancy: 15
Bathrooms: Two per building
Coed: Yes, single-sex by building
Residents: Upperclassmen
Room Types: Singles and doubles
Special Features: Meal plan requirement waived, house-like residences

Harwood
Floors: 4
Total Occupancy: 170
Bathrooms: Communal
Coed: Yes
Residents: Freshmen, sophomores
Room Types: Singles and doubles
Special Features: Laundy, kitchen, grand piano

Lawry
Floors: 3
Total Occupancy: 71
Bathrooms: Shared by suite
Coed: Yes
Residents: Upperclassmen
Room Types: Singles in eight-person suites
Special Features: Suite lounges, smoke-free living available

Lyon

Floors: 2
Total Occupancy: 75
Bathroom: Communal
Coed: Yes
Residents: Mostly freshmen
Room Types: Primarily doubles
Special Features: Lounge, kitchen, laundy

Mudd Blaisdell

Floors: 4
Total Occupancy: 280
Bathroom: Communal
Coed: Yes
Residents: Mostly freshmen
Room Types: Doubles and singles
Special Features: Air-conditioning, next to tennis courts and pool

Norton Clark

Floors: 3
Total Occupancy: 120
Bathrooms: Communal
Coed: Yes
Residents: Upperclassmen
Room Types: Primarily singles
Special Features: Three social rooms, courtyard access

Oldenborg

Floors: 3
Total Occupancy: 136
Bathrooms: Communal
Coed: Yes
Residents: Upperclassmen
Room Types: Primarily singles
Special Features: Language building, air-conditioning

Walker

Floors: 2
Total Occupancy: 112
Bathrooms: Communal
Coed: Yes
Residents: Mostly upperclassmen
Room Types: Singles and doubles
Special Features: Several lounges, grand piano, laundy, smoke free

Wig

Floors: 3
Total Occupancy: 113
Bathrooms: Communal
Coed: Yes
Residents: Mostly freshmen
Room Types: Singles and doubles
Special Features: Small patio, kitchen, laundry

Bed Type

Twin extra-long for all beds and some bunk beds

Available for Rent

MiniFridges and microwaves

Cleaning Service?

Public areas are cleaned weekly

What You Get

Each student receives a bed, desk, a dresser, two chairs, and Internet hookup

Also Available

Substance Free housing is available, but space is limited. There's also Quiet Hall, which is just what it sounds like: a hall with serious noise constraint rules.

Did You Know?

 Pomona's reputation of having "palatial" dorm rooms largely stems **from one or two big rooms with fireplaces** which you, in all likelihood, will never get to live in.

Smiley Dorm is the **oldest dorm west of the Mississippi River**. It's true—it's like living in a piece of history. The walls are so old and thin that once there was a minor earthquake, and they cracked. So, you might not want to try placing two mattresses opposite each other on the walls and bouncing between them, regardless of how fun it seems at first.

Students Speak Out On...
Campus Housing

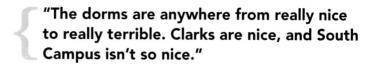

"The dorms are anywhere from really nice to really terrible. Clarks are nice, and South Campus isn't so nice."

Q "The dorms at Pomona are great. **There's a lot of variety**, and guaranteed four-year housing takes a lot of stress out of college life. There are 12 dorms on campus, and one is renovated every summer, so no dorm is more than 12 years old in terms of paint, furniture, and fixtures. South Campus dorms are where all the freshmen are; they generally are designed in 'rooms on a hallway' formats, which is good for meeting people. North Campus dorms are mostly upperclassmen and have a lot more singles, two-room double suites, and other interesting combinations."

Q "Dorms are **classy, renovated frequently, and well maintained**."

Q "The dorms are very nice. The rooms tend to be pretty big, and **the furniture is pretty nice, too**. Some dorms are really nice, but even the worst ones aren't completely bad by any means. Upperclassmen housing is practically palatial; some rooms have fireplaces and other amenities."

Q "For people who want singles, Walker or Clark 5 are the top choices. **For two-room doubles, Clark 1 is the way to go**. Smiley is the one dorm that is avoided like the plague; even though it's all singles, they are small, hot, and old. It needs to be renovated soon."

Q "The **dorms are beautiful**. Avoid Oldenborg your first year, though."

Q "I would say that the **underclassmen's dorms are nicer than those of the upperclassmen**, although I kind of liked the slightly seedy Spanish-style architecture on North Campus. The landscaping on North Campus is not particularly attractive, and the dorms can be rather loud on the weekends."

Q "The dorms are probably my biggest complaint about Pomona. Other residential colleges have interesting, varied housing options like theme-housing, co-ops, and senior apartments. **At Pomona, it's just singles, doubles, divided doubles**, and the really awful language dorm, Oldenborg."

Q "Dorms are **fairly nice**. They desperately need air-conditioning, though!"

Q "The dorms are good. Even though **freshman housing generally involves sharing a small room** with a complete stranger, that is going to be the same almost anywhere you go. After freshman year, most people can get singles if they really want one or group together with friends in friendship suites. On-campus housing, overall, is pretty nice."

Q "The dorms are mostly **gorgeous and unique**, but there is a disturbing trend of removing the character of each dorm when it is renovated. This has also happened to a lot of the gardens."

Q "I've had a single since freshman year. Very nice on the whole, except for the first month of the school year, when **it's deathly hot** and most dorms have no air-conditioning. Bring a fan. Actually, bring two."

Q "Housing here is **fabulous**. There are some of the nicest dorms I have ever seen."

Q "Be sure to **visit your prospective room before you draw for it**. Avoid Harwood 189, as its only window opens onto a concrete stairwell. You should also try to avoid the room next to the dormitory door. When people are too drunk to operate the card scanners, they will often pound on the nearest window until somebody comes out."

The College Prowler Take On...
Campus Housing

Pomona's dorms are an eclectic bunch, and opinions regarding how nice they are vary widely. Something particularly nice about Pomona is that it is relatively easy to get a single if you want one. This can have all kinds of advantages, aside from the obvious romantic ones. However, there are some often overlooked benefits to having a roommate. It can be a valuable learning experience to live with someone else; you must learn to curb your habits, and you might gain that sought after mark of maturity known as acceptance. Also, you won't get lonely with a roommate, and you'll find it easier to meet people as well. What many underclassmen don't realize is that ,to get the really nice rooms (the big ones with fireplaces and personal balconies) you must nearly always sacrifice the option of having a single as a senior. If you want a single but still want to be close to your friends, you may end up with a balcony or a courtyard, but the interiors of your rooms will resemble the interiors of tenement housing. For many, the choice between having a single and having a really nice room can be a tough one.

Dorms here are constantly being renovated, and as such, they tend to be relatively clean and well-appointed. As 97% of Pomona students live on campus all four years of college, the College places high priority on forming a "residential community."

B+

The College Prowler® Grade on
Campus Housing: B+

A high Campus Housing grade indicates that dorms are clean, well-maintained, and spacious. Other determining factors include variety of dorms, proximity to classes, and social atmosphere.

Off-Campus Housing

The Lowdown On...
Off-Campus Housing

Undergrads in Off-Campus Housing:
3%

Average Rent For:
Studio Apt.: $400/month
1BR Apt.: $700/month
2BR Apt.: $800/month

Popular Areas:
The outskirts of the Village
The Claremont Pacifica

For Assistance Contact:
CGU (Claremont Graduate University) housing services
www.cgu.edu
(909) 607-2609

Best Time to Look for a Place:
Late summer or late spring

Students Speak Out On...
Off-Campus Housing

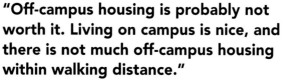

"Off-campus housing is probably not worth it. Living on campus is nice, and there is not much off-campus housing within walking distance."

Q "I heard **97 percent of people live on campus**. I don't know anyone who lives off campus, and I don't know where the people who do actually live."

Q "It's **not convenient** to live off campus."

Q "I don't really know anything about it, but it seems like **most people live on campus for a reason**."

Q "**It's not convenient to live off campus**. I don't know whether it's worth it. If you have a pleasant, cooperative, and reasonably responsible roommate, then living off campus lets you retain some semblance of a social life while freeing you psychologically from being a student all the time. Some people need this."

Q "Living off campus is really **only practical if you have a car**; though apartments and rooms for rent exist within a 20-minute walking distance from campus, there aren't that many. Figuring out what to do with the apartment during the summer can be a preclusive pain in the butt. In addition, most Pomona students prefer to remain on campus, so finding a roommate can be tricky."

Q "Almost everyone at Pomona lives on campus **for all four years**."

Q "I don't know where people live off campus, or **why they even bother**."

Q "Students are **forbidden to live off campus** until their sophomore year, and then they have to make a special request which can be denied, depending on whether the college has filled its dorms with paying students."

Q "Most students **never live off campus**, and most students love living in the dorms. It forces them to live next to the most random weirdoes who eventually become friends. Plus, it's nice to be spoon-fed, or not to have to worry about making food, cleaning, or making the time to visit friends."

Q "If you hate campus, which some students do, then **living off campus is worth it**. However, most life at Pomona is campus based, so living off campus you can miss out on a lot."

Q "It's **not too convenient** and not worth it."

The College Prowler Take On...
Off-Campus Housing

About 97 percent of Pomona students live on campus for all four years of their college career. There are a number of reasons for this. For one, off-campus housing is expensive and hard to find, and most affordable places are too far away for you to really feel like you are "part of the college community." Also, it's just so darned convenient to live on campus. The whole campus is only five by six blocks, and everything you need is provided for you. There is a small off-campus scene, largely revolving around a few traditionally passed down college houses in the Village, such as "Harvard House" and the "cottages," which are four campus-owned houses in the Village for sophomores, but the options are severely limited.

Housing off campus is pricey and inaccessible, and all but the most intrepid students take the path of least resistance and opt to live on campus. Of course, some take the road less traveled and hitch their wagon to an off-campus star. These iconoclasts have a hard row to hoe, and unless they are very social, it can be far too easy to get stranded off campus, and cut off from the daily goings on which are so integral to the Pomona experience. Such people might feel akin to the first simian cosmonauts, floating in their tiny, tin spacecraft, alone, adrift, and surrounded by the eternal blackness of space. Then again, some may not feel this way at all. With perseverance and a courageous heart, you can forge a life for yourself in the brave new world of off campus without abandoning your Pomona roots. The average Pomona student, however, is lazy and would find the amount of work required so far in excess of any possible reward that they would hardly even consider the option.

D-

The College Prowler® Grade on

Off-Campus
Housing: D-

A high grade in Off-Campus Housing indicates that apartments are of high quality, close to campus, affordable, and easy to secure.

Diversity

The Lowdown On...
Diversity

Native American:
Less than 1%

White:
70%

Asian American:
13%

International:
2%

African American:
6%

Out-of-State:
63%

Hispanic:
9%

Political Activity

Pomona is a hotbed of student protest. There is nearly always someone protesting something. From poor worker conditions in the dining hall to the sale of the Bernard Field Station to a biotech institute, Pomona students stay active politically, and they are excellent enactors of the motto: "Think globally, act locally."

Gay Pride

Generally Pomona is a very accepting environment; there is a QRC (Queer Resource Center), a Queer and Questioning club, and there are many queer-sponsored activities on campus. Most gay students do not find discrimination to be a major factor in their lives.

Economic Status

Pretty rich, generally. You won't, however, find a bunch of old-moneyed, eastern snobs here. Instead, you will find a bunch of new-moneyed, western snobs cleverly, but imperfectly, disguised as laid-back hippies.

Minority Clubs

Asian Pacific Islander Awareness Committee, Asian American Students Association, Chinese Student Association, Hui Laule'a, Hawaiian students' organization, International Club, International/Intercultural Association, Jewish Student Union, Korean Students Association, Movimiento Estudiantil Chicano de Aztlan (MEChA), Muslim Students' Association, Pan-African Students Association, Unidos, Vietnamese American Student Association, World Youth Network

Most Popular Religions

Most Pomona students are either Protestant, Catholic, or Jewish.

Students Speak Out On...
Diversity

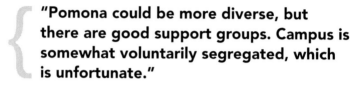

> **"Pomona could be more diverse, but there are good support groups. Campus is somewhat voluntarily segregated, which is unfortunate."**

Q "Campus is pretty diverse. Students are primarily **white and Asian**, but there are decent representations of other minorities."

Q "Supposedly it's diverse, but **different groups don't mingle a lot**, in my opinion. I'm white, as are most of my friends, with few exceptions. It's not that I prefer hanging out with only white people, but I hardly ever see Asian or black people socially."

Q "The racial percentages look pretty good. However, the class seems homogenous in its desire not to rock the boat. In addition, Pomona has very **few international students**."

Q "I think it's really diverse, but I'm from Alaska, **so my standards may be skewed**. I think most people can't be boxed in, and everyone brings a bit of flavor to Pomona."

Q "Pomona's campus has a **very diverse mix of upper and upper-middle class, white people** with a few token minorities thrown in. This can be a little intimidating for someone who has, for instance, never seen a black person before, but for the most part there is nothing to be afraid of. The minorities at Pomona largely either act like white people or keep to themselves."

Q "Despite the numbers, the campus is **not very diverse**, unless you count the housekeeping and maintenance staff."

Q "The campus is **considerably less diverse than the surrounding community** and the nation at large. There are different kinds of diversity—racial, sexual, biological, ecological, geographical—and Pomona can boast only approximately equal numbers of men and women."

Q "Students are **mostly Caucasian**, but I've met many international students and some students with unique backgrounds.

Q "The campus is diverse for a very selective liberal arts college. However, **many social and racial groups are still underrepresented**."

Q "People's ethnic backgrounds are somewhat diverse for a college in Pomona's category, but **there is little diversity** in people's values, socioeconomic status, or political stances."

The College Prowler Take On...
Diversity

Pomona's numbers concerning campus diversity come out looking pretty good, but the majority of students don't feel that the school is really all that diverse. Cited lack of socio-economic variance and a prevalence of ideological conformity tend to account for this impression. Pomona does have a good representation of different ethnicities, and it is very accepting of its students, regardless of their background or views. Many, however, wish that there could be a better representation as far as experience goes. Black or white, gay or straight, most Pomona kids come from upper-middle-class suburban American backgrounds, and as such, their differences are viewed by many as only skin deep.

Students here fall pretty safely in the middle of most spectra. We tend to think what college students are supposed to think, do what they do, say what they say, and so on. This is not necessarily a bad thing; Pomona's environment is amazingly comfortable for many students, and there are many wonderful, unique people here. However, there is an easy way to define diversity and a hard way, and Pomona tends to opt for the former. We all know diversity is "good," but often it is far simpler to throw a bone to the dogs of political correctness than it is to let loose the dogs of culture-clash.

The College Prowler® Grade on
Diversity: C+

A high grade in Diversity indicates that ethnic minorities and international students have a notable presence on campus and that students of different economic backgrounds, religious beliefs, and sexual preferences are well-represented.

Guys & Girls

The Lowdown On...
Guys & Girls

Men Undergrads:
50%

Women Undergrads:
50%

Birth Control Available?

There are free condoms in the health hut, and morning-after pills are available as well.

Social Scene

The social scene largely revolves around drinking and school clubs and activities. Generally, people who do their socializing while drinking do so almost every night. People who go more in for the activities side of things might party on the weekend, but will tend to spend their weekdays doing a variety of things (rock climbing, surfing, macramé, student government, organic gardening). This is, of course, merely a rough distinction. It is pretty easy to meet people if you stay active, but often there are complaints about how difficult it is to establish really close, intimate, meaningful friendships here.

Hookups or Relationships?

Both are prevalent. There is the common liberal arts school lament that no one dates, and of course, no one dates. Everyone already knows everyone else. If dating is an essential part of your plans for college, this isn't the place to come. Of course, if you were of an open mind, you could look at the process of hooking up as a sort of dating for the 21st century. It's like extreme dating; you only have about two alcohol-soused hours to really get to know someone and travel the desired amount of metaphorical bases. In this analog, the long term "relationships" that occasionally spring out of repeated hookups with same person constitute "going steady." There; the '50s are alive and well at Pomona. If all this is too retro-avant-garde for you, you can always traditionally date some older person from the Village. This is, however, often looked down upon.

Best Place to Meet Guys/Girls

Big parties, generally. While the majority of Pomona romance stems from the repetitive random hookups, and these almost always happen at parties, it is important to remember that it's during your day to day routine that the seeds for these social interactions are sown. After all, if you've exchanged blushing glances over your books in chemistry class, you're a lot more likely to end up exchanging blushing glances in a somewhat less formal environment. On the other hand, too many blushing glances and you might just end up being friends. This is no uncommon occurrence at Pomona, where it is arguably way too easy to hang out with someone you like, thus disarming the potentially-explosive apparatus that is sexual tension.

Dress Code

Very casual with lots of pajamas, sandals, and the occasional muumuu. Pomona is not a mecca of fashion, although females seem to have a lot of expensive shoes and bags.

Did You Know?

Top Places to Find Hotties:

1. Any of Pomona's many themed "dress-so-scantily-that-if-we-were-anywhere-but-a-privately-owned-gated-community-we-would-all-be-arrested-for-exposure" parties.

2. Econ classes for the more made-up and buttoned down crowd, poly-sci for the conformist but not square, and English or theater classes for the slightly more experimental.

3. Table Manners!

4. (Not the library! I don't know where Pomona students do their studying, but the library is full of CGU students, who tend to be in their 30s and married.)

Top Places to Hook Up:

1. The top of the bell tower (this, of course, requires a key.)

2. The stage on the Greek Theater late at night (for the particularly daring.)

3. Pretty much any corner of any building holding any party on any Friday or Saturday.

4. The Montgomery Gallery roof (very accessible, and arguably a "cultural" experience.)

5. The swimming pool after hours (but you have to be quick, because there are laser-tripped alarms, and Campus Security responds promptly.)

Students Speak Out On...
Guys & Girls

"The girls are by no means hot, although on the plus side a lot of them are rich. I've heard the guys are not much better."

 "Everyone here is **kind of nerdy**, or used to be nerdy and now wants to pretend that they never were. That means we get a lot of variety in types of people and personalities. We have a saying, 'There is No Sex at Pomona College.' I mean, there is, but generally, it seems people are too shy to start things."

"The **girls are pretty good**, but it appears that most don't really care how they look. After the first month of school, they break out the sweatpants and forget how to apply makeup. It's not the University of Arizona, that's for sure."

"**My boyfriend's really hot**, but the rest of the student body is mainly middling. If you have a fetish for pale, weedy intellectuals, you're in luck. My boyfriend's pale and intellectual, but he's not weedy."

"Everyone here is **pretty attractive**. I don't know why it's like a black hole of hotness. Of course, I'm attractive, so I may be biased."

"All the hipster guys with bands graduated, I think. They were so, so hot! But **there are some cool girls left**, and we are hot, too!"

Q "There are **plenty of beautiful people**, but in general, students dress very casually and don't wear a lot of makeup."

Q "Umm. Let's just say **your standards lower**."

Q "They're hot as first-years, and then **they all get fat and old**."

Q "People are pretty laid-back, and generally attractive, but with few students, **the 'menu' can seem pretty barren, sometimes**."

Q "The girls don't wear much makeup and don't generally seem to have too many eating disorders. **The boys are mostly lame**. It doesn't seem that anyone was particularly hot at Pomona. Everyone is absorbed by the Pomona sludge and becomes ugly. It will happen to you."

Q "The **guys are mostly nerdy people or bland**, passionless, fantasy baseball jocks. The girls study way too much and aren't very hot when they do get dressed up for parties anyway."

Q "Lots of hot girls, **lack of hot guys**. Most of the hot guys are gay!"

The College Prowler Take On...
Guys & Girls

It is a generally accepted fact that Pomona students just don't care that much about how they look. Freshmen have hold-over fashion sense from high school, but this is quickly sapped by the general aesthetic apathy of the student body. This is not to say that people here are ugly, because they're not. They tend to stay relatively active and in shape, and most of them aren't from the shallowest end of the gene pool. They just care more about drinking and hanging out than making devastating impressions on their chosen sexual targets. This makes a lot of sense when you think about the fact that everyone knows everyone else.

Pomona's dating scene is pretty non-existent, but there is an awful lot of hooking up. If you just want to find a nice boy or girl who is willing to take things slow, have lemonade with your parents, and who blushes fetchingly when you hold hands, then you had best hope there is an eligible person in your sponsor group, because that's one of the only ways such relationships get spawned, and/or stand a chance of lasting at Pomona. But remember, "sponcest," although not illegal in the state of California, is heavily stigmatized, and all that social pressure can tear through a relationship like an acetylene torch through a tin can. Oh, but don't fret; the tale of sex at Pomona isn't entirely grim. Remember that alcohol is really just another name for "aphrodisiac."

The College Prowler® Grade on
Guys: C+

A high grade for Guys indicates that the male population on campus is attractive, smart, friendly, and engaging, and that the school has a decent ratio of guys to girls.

The College Prowler® Grade on
Girls: B

A high grade for Girls not only implies that the women on campus are attractive, smart, friendly, and engaging, but also that there is a fair ratio of girls to guys.

Athletics

The Lowdown On...
Athletics

Athletic Division:
Division III

Conference:
SCIAC (Southern California Intercollegiate Athletic Conference)

School Mascot:
Cecil Sagehen

Males Playing Varsity Sports:
183 (16%)

Females Playing Varsity Sports:
134 (10%)

➜

Men's Varsity Sports:

Baseball
Basketball
Cross-Country
Football
Golf
Soccer
Swimming & Diving
Tennis
Track & Field
Water Polo

Women's Varsity Sports:

Basketball
Cross-Country
Golf
Soccer
Softball
Swimming & Diving
Tennis
Track & Field
Volleyball
Water Polo

Club Sports:

Badminton
Ballroom Dance
Lacrosse (Men's and Women's)
Rugby (Men's and Women's)
Ultimate Frisbee (Men's and Women's)
Volleyball (Men's)

Intramurals:

Innertube Water Polo
Table Tennis
Racquetball
Indoor Soccer
Basketball
Tennis

Athletic Fields

Fully-renovated baseball, football, and soccer fields, 14 all-weather tennis courts, an eight-lane, all-weather track, and numerous practice fields

Getting Tickets

Not necessary

Most Popular Sports

Rugby, soccer, football, and baseball

Best Place to Take a Walk

South Campus—around the track and the nature preserve

Gyms/Facilities

Rains Center for Sport and Recreation

The Rains Center is Pomona's main athletic facility. It boasts numerous basketball and volleyball courts, as well as a fully-equipped weight training room, saunas, and training rooms. The main complaint is that it closes awfully early.

Students Speak Out On...
Athletics

"Many people play varsity sports, but I wouldn't say that they're big. At Pomona, you don't really get any prestige for being an athlete. I don't know much about IM sports."

Q "Sports are **not that important here**. We are Division III. Most of the teams have good years and bad years. People go to games not so much because we're good, but because they know everyone on the team. IM sports are popular. Some of the IM options include ultimate Frisbee, flag football, and inner tube water polo."

Q "Varsity sports are **fairly big**, and many people participate in them."

Q "Varsity sports **don't receive a lot of emphasis at Pomona**. If you have a friend, you generally go see him or her play, but huge crowds are not the norm unless teams are playing CMC (the across campus rival). IM sports on the other hand are very popular and a lot of fun."

Q "Sports here are **big to those who play them**, and to all the rest, they are just so-so."

Q "I went to a Pomona football game once. **It was okay**."

Q "Sports are **somewhat of a joke**. Pomona thankfully doesn't take itself seriously enough to recruit any nefarious testosterone-laden dunces."

Q *"**No one gives a damn** about sports here."*

Q *"**Pomona sucks at sports**. Though the women's tennis team is actually supposed to be pretty good. The nice thing about Pomona being so small is that anyone can participate in a sport if she or he wants without being a 'college athlete.' There is lots of room for people who just do sports as hobbies."*

The College Prowler Take On...
Athletics

As a small Division III school, Pomona doesn't put that much emphasis on athletics. Some of the sports are taken pretty seriously, however, particularly football, baseball, basketball, track, soccer, and rugby (If anyone can take seriously a sport that requires you to drink a sweaty shoe-full of beer whenever you score a "try".) The varsity athletes do get very involved in their sports and are often somewhat cliquish, but general student support and interest is relatively low. Athletes tend to attend the games of other athletes. Some intramural sports, such as ultimate Frisbee and innertube water polo, generate a fair amount of excitement, as well.

If it is important to you that you be worshipped on the basis of your athletic might and main, then don't come to Pomona. You will not be worshipped. You might be some coach's sweaty dream embodied, but don't let him or her trick you into thinking sports here are all that important. Most students care about as much for sports as they do for any club or activity that they aren't involved in. "Polite disinterest" would be a good way to characterize their feelings. No one's going to look down on you for grunting and knocking heads with your testosterone-dripping cronies, but they aren't likely to ask for a signed jock strap either. That said, Pomona has a perfectly respectable athletic program for a Division III school, and there are plenty of opportunities for sport at the college. Football is really the only sport that gets any recruiting power.

The College Prowler® Grade on

Athletics: C+

A high grade in Athletics indicates that students have school spirit, that sports programs are respected, that games are well-attended, and that intramurals are a prominent part of student life.

Nightlife

The Lowdown On...
Nightlife

Club & Bar Prowler: Popular Nightlife Spots!

Club Prowler:

There are no clubs in this area.

Bar Prowler:

Black Watch Pub

497 N Central Ave.
Upland, CA 91786

(909) 981-6069

(Black Watch Pub, continued)

Black Wwatch is very popular with the Pomona crowd, primarily because of the large tap selection and live local bands.

Friar Tucks Bar & Grille

540 E Foothill Blvd.
Pomona, CA 91767

(909) 625-7265

Friar Tucks is also a good place to catch live bands, both local bands and smaller national ones. For listings of their upcoming shows, check out *www.jambase.com*.

Heroes Restaurant

131 Yale Ave.
Claremont, CA 91711

(909) 621-6712

As popular for their food as their drinks, Heroes is a great spot to kick back and watch sports, and they even sell bagged peanuts like you're at the ballgame.

The Hi Brow

547 E Foothill Blvd.
Pomona, CA 91767

(909) 626-9340

Hi Brow is Pomona's basic dive bar, and all Pomona students probably pass through these doors at one time or another. It is one of the last bars in California in which you can still smoke.

Student Favorites:
Pomona parties, or if there's a good band playing, The Blackwatch Pub or Friar Tucks.

Other Places to Check Out:
Los Angeles

Bars Close At:
2 a.m.

Primary Areas with Nightlife:
Los Angeles or anywhere off of Foothill Blvd.

Cheapest Place to Get a Drink:
Black Watch Pub on College Nights

Favorite Drinking Games:
Flip-Cup
Caps
Boat Race

Useful Resources for Nightlife:
http://gocalifornia.about.com/cs/nightlife

What to Do if You're Not 21

Sit at home and cry into your non-alcoholic near-beer. Or you could take part in one of the myriad non-alcoholic activities and events at Pomona. There isn't any shortage. Fake IDs have become harder to construct now that the ID style has changed.

Local Specialties

Heroes, although expensive, has something like 67 beers on tap. Also, you can eat peanuts and throw the shells on the floor, which may account for the bar's "B" health rating.

Organization Parties

The Bathroom Party – A Pomona college legend, the bathroom party is hosted by Nu Alpha Phi, the "hippie" frat. When it began, it was held in a different bathroom on campus each year. The theme was simple: come as naked as you can handle, cross dressing being an alternative for those not comfortable baring it all. The party grew in popularity and attendance, and in the last few years has been held in Grooveline, Pomona's on-campus club room, also home to the always-well-attended Thursday night Junior/Senior Social. With the suspension of the Nappies' charter, the future of the bathroom party is uncertain.

Harwood Halloween – It used to be held in the Harwood courtyard and was consistently ranked among *Playboy* magazine's top 10 college parties. Now, it's held up on North Campus and gets shut down within a half an hour nearly every year. The problem is that Pomona gets a big-name band and gives them a big-time sound system, and the quiet, early-to-bed Claremont residents get big-time angry.

(Organization Parties, continued)

Desert parties – Also often hosted by Nu Alpha Phi, although occasionally hosted by non-college-affiliated organizations, these parties involve a huge generator and a DJ, and all-night-long rave music in the uninhabited, deep desert. Drug use is common, but certainly not required. However, before heading out to the back country, remember that running around in the desert at night in your right mind can get pretty old when you're freezing and hungry to begin with, then boiling and burning and starving, and your ride is having such an excellent time, and is so exstatic, that he can't exactly find it in his heart to head back until every other saggy-eyed, sand-chapped hippie has left.

Frats

See the Greek section!

Students Speak Out On...
Nightlife

"Parties on campus are good, with free alcohol. Off campus, well, LA is not too far away and has lots of opportunities for nighttime fun as long as you have access to a car."

Q "Parties on campus **happen quite often**. The school organizes parties and weekend activities though campus organizations like ASPC and CCLA. We have annual, elaborately-themed parties like the Lei Party, Harwood Halloween, and Smiley '80s. Those are just a few of the most popular. Harwood Halloween was actually rated by *Playboy* magazine a few years ago as being one of the top five college parties in the country. The school also offers a lot of alcohol-free activities, like swim and movie nights, or trips to laser-tag places in town. There aren't really any bars in town, and I don't know of any clubs in the area."

Q "Parties are **alcohol-filled and sometimes fun**. It depends what kind of thing you like. There are also some smokey dive bars that people frequent. But most people tend to stay on campus and party there, strangely enough."

Q "Campus parties **tend to be pretty fun**, although they can get monotonous. It's usually a DJ and two or three kegs. Sometimes, they check IDs. Sometimes, they don't. There is a fair amount of partying in the dorms. A lot of times, people will start in the dorms and then move to the official school party. I don't know much about off-campus stuff, but there are a couple of dive bars about a five-minute drive away that are pretty cheap, if you get sick of the on-campus stuff. Usually, though, campus is the place to be."

Q "Parties on campus are fun, **lots of people go**, while bars are close and pretty cheap, but kind of shady."

Q "There are **no good bars near campus**! The city of Claremont seems set against providing the students with a convenient, satisfying night life. The Black Watch Pub is nice, but it's a bit of a drive to get there. Ditto for Friar Tuck's, except for the 'nice' bit. The College offers free 'safe rides' from any off-campus event to campus any day of the week. Safe Ride is only a semi-helpful service, because it doesn't help you get out to the event in the first place."

Q "Uh, **I recommend smaller parties in people's rooms**, but some of the bigger ones are all right too, I guess."

Q "Parties on campus have **free beer, bump 'n' grind music, and a fair amount of easy, drunk girls**. If this is not your scene, you could also hang out in your room and get high. There are few good bars in the area, and Pomona students generally do not venture into the outlying areas."

Q "The best parties on campus surround the Tuesday night event 'Table Manners.' The event itself is open to everyone, and it's a good time to dance and have free beer and sometimes wine, but **the best are the small, very exclusive, occasionally-orgiastic parties** afterward."

Q "Most partying at Pomona takes place on campus. **The college funds large dance parties** pretty much every weekend. Students generally gather in each others' rooms to pre-party (get drunk, flirt, and so on) before going out to the 5C (five college) parties. The 5C parties vary in attendance and quality with some flopping and others drawing thousands of people."

Q "Parties are **fun for the first couple of years**, but by the end, they begin to feel like freshman meat-markets. Alcohol is always available."

Q "Parties on campus are **great because the alcohol is free**, but they get old after the first year, seeming to always be stretching for a theme so as to seem like a unique party. But then, by senior year, they take on an ironic and sentimental value, and they become fun again. I feel like the people who planned them were on the prom committee in high school and have no idea what a good time really is, but you always make your own fun."

Q "Bars and clubs: **you can't walk anywhere good in less than 20 minutes**, but just a little further, there are some good dives, like the Hi Brow. The Inland Empire's cheesy gay club, Oasis, is in a strip mall and looks like a bar from *Top Gun* on the inside. It's very popular with the locals, but students rarely go out. It forces them to leave their new-found security of campus life; most students at Pomona were unpopular in high school and are finally finding themselves socially comfortable at Pomona, so they rarely leave that security blanket to experience the real world."

Q "There are **only dives off campus** if you don't want to go to the on-campus parties."

The College Prowler Take On...
Nightlife

Pomona is one of the happiest colleges in the country. There are those who credit this to the somewhat astronomical amount of free beer available on campus. Religion may or may not be the opiate of the masses, but it's pretty clear that free beer is the opiate of the college student. The beer is distributed five or six nights a week to anybody with a valid or well-faked ID. As for the Village, there are two bars, Heroes, "where good friends meet," (well, to be fair, I did meet with some good friends there once, but only once) and Pizza 'N Such (I guess the "'N Such" is liquor), which tries pretty hard to cater to college students, and actually has a full bar (but isn't the best place to get crazy drunk, as there are often families in there eating pizza). And of course, there's always LA.

If you don't have very stringent expectations for your nightlife, Pomona will do just fine. There are tons of parties (especially with the other four colleges right there) and a ton of alcohol, dancing, and hooking up. Sometimes, though, this can be a little tiresome. At Pomona, even the most easily-entertained and creative students will eventually run out of options for entertainment. Fortunately, history repeats, and in the grand recourse of Pomona College, all old things shall be made new again. Or whatever.

B-

The College Prowler® Grade on

Nightlife: B-

A high grade in Nightlife indicates that there are many bars and clubs in the area that are easily accessible and affordable. Other determining factors include the number of options for the under-21 crowd and the prevalence of house parties.

Greek Life

The Lowdown On...
Greek Life

Number of Fraternities:
3

Number of Sororities:
0

Undergrad Men in Fraternities:
5%

Undergrad Women in Sororities:
0%

→

Fraternities:

Kappa Delta

Nu Alpha Phi (coed)

Sigma Tau

Sororities:

None

Multicultural Colonies:

None

Did You Know?

The extent of the fraternity facilities on campus pretty much consist of "the Boot," the site of their **weekly keggers** and home to some of the biggest, nastiest cockroaches I have ever had the misfortune to lay eyes on.

Although the frats aren't always exactly welcoming to non-brothers, it is in their charter that their parties must be open to all, so **they really have no choice but to let you drink their beer**, which they bought with their own funds. Really, though, once you get to know them, many of them are truly wonderful individuals.

Students Speak Out On...
Greek Life

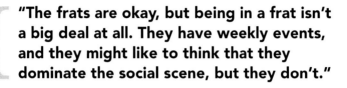

"The frats are okay, but being in a frat isn't a big deal at all. They have weekly events, and they might like to think that they dominate the social scene, but they don't."

Q "Sororities are **not allowed on campus** due to a fund donated by this old lady that provides for fresh flowers on all the dining hall tables so long as no sororities are ever allowed to establish themselves."

Q "[Greek life at Pomona is] Non-existent. As of now, we have one 'true' frat on campus, but since they don't have frat housing, they're more like a club. **They're kind of lame**; they party on Tuesday nights and lob water balloons at people off the Mudd-Blaisdell roof."

Q "The **Greeks belong to the cult of Dionysus**, which works out for the rest of us because we get to partake of the libations too. But, I only did it twice because the people, fun, and alcohol cocktails was one heady mix that I tried to avoid on weekdays, in case my head exploded. I suspect guys join frats so that they can flick wet towels at each other in the locker room and not be accused of flirting."

Q "**My roommate took a Greek class** once, and from what I heard, it was pretty good. It did dominate his life for a time, but he really seemed to get a lot out of it, so I would not consider that a negative thing really."

Q "**Greek life at Pomona is a complete joke**. At least one frat realizes that and has a somewhat ironic self-awareness. The other two are just pathetic."

Q "**Greek life is a joke**. There are two fraternities that are not even part of the Greek system. One of them has the same name as a national sorority, and the other one pretty much just gets high and drunk amongst themselves. It is perfectly possible to party at Pomona for four years without ever attending a Greek function."

Q "I wouldn't know. **I have never been to Greece**."

Q "There **isn't very much Greek life**. In fact, if you take part in Greek life, you're considered pathetic."

Q "Frat life **doesn't dominate the social scene**, thank heavens!"

The College Prowler Take On...
Greek Life

Greek life at Pomona is indeed severely limited. Many wonder why it even exists. It is largely due to the patronage of one Fred Sontag, Pomona philosophy professor, who has always been a strong proponent of frats as a place for young men to, essentially, be young men together. That's pretty much how it works. Kappa Delta and Sigma Tau both host a weekly kegger, but neither have houses of their own. Attendance at the events is generally somewhat limited. Nu Alpha Phi is a coed frat and is responsible for a number of the wilder, stranger campus events, but they don't have a house either, and they really don't resemble a frat in anything but name.

If you want to be involved in Greek life at Pomona, just don't expect it to be like *Animal House*. They may, or may not, be animals, but they don't have a house, so the frats' place on campus is basically limited to their weekly keggers. Sometimes, they hold fundraisers, like the Kappa Delta "buy a date with a Kappa Delta guy" thing. There are a significant handful of non-frat students who take advantage of the frat events, either for the beer or for the purpose of flirting with frat boys.

The College Prowler® Grade on
Greek Life: D+

A high grade in Greek Life indicates that sororities and fraternities are not only present, but also active on campus. Other determining factors include the variety of houses available and the respect the Greek community receives from the rest of the campus.

Drug Scene

The Lowdown On...
Drug Scene

Most Prevalent Drugs on Campus:

Alcohol

Ecstasy

Marijuana

Liquor-Related Referrals:

4

Liquor-Related Arrests:

0

Drug-Related Referrals:

0

Drug-Related Arrests:

1

Drug Counseling Programs:

The College refers students to AA, and short-term individual counseling and theme-based group counseling are available from the Monsour Counseling Center.

(909) 621-8222

Students Speak Out On...
Drug Scene

> **"I've never encountered anything harder than weed or 'shrooms. People do it, but it's not socially mandatory."**

 "There are **quite a few people who smoke pot**, but there are very few 'potheads.' Hard drugs are very rare. Alcohol is common, but people are generally responsible about it and only drink on weekends."

"The drug scene is **pretty normal as colleges go**. You won't encounter what you don't want to encounter, and what you want, you can pretty much find."

"I probably shouldn't comment because I don't know much, but I think there is **definitely marijuana** and alcohol around. I imagine that there is harder stuff going on, but it's definitely not pervasive."

"**I heard a lot of people were into cocaine** my freshman year, then I heard that it wasn't 'in' anymore, and it all but disappeared. People seem to smoke a lot of marijuana so that you'd think that that was 'the' drug on campus. Personally, I think there are quite a few people who prefer popping pills and quite a few people who enjoy harder drugs, too."

"**The dealer who was everyone's dealer got busted**. So, the drug scene is sort of in transition."

"The drug scene was **bigger in my high school**; aside from pot, drugs are pretty hard to come by."

Q "If you want something, **you can usually find it**."

Q "The drug use I have witnessed has been primarily **limited to tobacco, alcohol, and marijuana**. Some students also use mushrooms and acid, and I have heard about but never witnessed the use of cocaine."

Q "There's **lots of pot**. Get some if you can. Pomona's the perfect place to experiment. I only wish I had done more of it while I was there."

Q "Oh, the drug scene is **happening** if you want it to be."

The College Prowler Take On...
Drug Scene

Well, the fact is just about any drug one desires is available on campus, but they're not a highly visible part of campus life. Tons of people drink, and many smoke pot, but there are also select pockets of the student body who use other drugs, as well. Ecstasy is big sometimes, as are 'shrooms and acid. Cocaine is available, but only the richest use it with anything approaching regularity. Lots of students use pills as study aids, at least that's what they claim the pills are for, but harder stuff like meth or heroin is almost non-existent on campus. The conventional wisdom is that if you want to find a drug or a group of people who use a certain drug, you'll probably be successful, but if you don't, except for beer (and sometimes pot), you really won't have much experience with other drugs. Users tend to be somewhat responsible, and very circumspect, which is largely because the College is incredibly tolerant about pot and alcohol and hard on anything else.

Drugs aren't a necessity for a social life at Pomona; as often as not, they're an escape from a sometimes overwhelmingly-present social scene. Alcohol and pot are definitely mainstays of the social scene, but not the entire social scene. They can certainly be avoided if you want (especially if you live in substance-free hall), but other drug use is generally geared toward escapism. The very fact that some students can attend Pomona for four years and be active and social and still have no idea of the extent to which drug use pervades the campus is proof positive that it's not generally that big of a deal. However, the grade would be higher save the prevalence of alcohol on campus.

The College Prowler® Grade on
Drug Scene: B-

A high grade in the Drug Scene indicates that drugs are not a noticeable part of campus life; drug use is not visible, and no pressure to use them seems to exist.

Campus Strictness

The Lowdown On...
Campus Strictness

What Are You Most Likely to Get Caught Doing on Campus?

- Stealing a golf cart (don't take them off campus or the College will call the Claremont Police)
- Breaking stuff.
- Climbing trees—despite the wealth of tantalizing trees adorning the grounds of Pomona college, attempts to climb them are met by the security guards with a pointed finger and a stern head-wag, and sometimes, with the words: "You! Uh-uh."

Students Speak Out On...
Campus Strictness

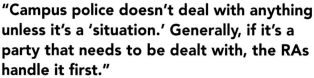

"Campus police doesn't deal with anything unless it's a 'situation.' Generally, if it's a party that needs to be dealt with, the RAs handle it first."

Q "Don't be excessively stupid and **you won't have any problems**."

Q "The campus is **not very strict**, unless you do something really stupid or damage stuff. As long as you're being safe, Campus Security will pretty much leave you alone. They are definitely a presence. You see them pretty often on weekend nights."

Q "Generally, **if you stay cool, the RAs will stay cool**. We have a concept here that involves public versus private space. Generally, if it's contained in your room or behind a closed door, you're fine."

Q "One time, I was asked by Campus Security to **pour out my beer** when I was drinking in public."

Q "Campus Security really **won't interfere** with your personal freedoms at college, unless some jerk narcs on you."

Q "The Campus Security realizes that **students mostly know how to handle themselves**, except the dumb freshman girls who add to the alcohol-poisoning stats at least once every week."

Q "The campus police are **amazingly lax concerning the drinking and drugs**. Essentially, anything done behind closed doors in a dorm room without creating a ridiculous level of noise will go undisturbed. Even outside of the dorm rooms, Campus Safety is quite relaxed. While I was walking around campus with a full beer in my hand, a member of Campus Safety once told me that I had 'better chug that or pour it out.'"

Q "The security guards are **getting stricter by the year**."

Q "I always thought it was kind of a **'don't see don't tell' policy**."

Q "Security is pretty **lax**."

The College Prowler Take On...
Campus Strictness

A favorite word for Campus Security's level of strictness is "lax," which pretty much speaks for itself. Campus Security officers are more concerned with safety than with being policemen. They aren't out to ruin people's fun. There are always rumors of certain officers partying with students, but most of them play it pretty safe. One thing Pomona tries to be harsh on is vandalism, which has become an increasing problem in the last few years. So while a Campus Security officer might very well turn a blind eye to your not-so-incognito brown-bagged forty, he or she is not likely to turn the same blind eye to your attempts to break a dorm window with your head.

The most common cause for parties getting shut down at Pomona is a noise complaint. Generally, if there is a lot of noise being made anytime after quiet hours, some spoil sport (or maybe a perfectly nice person who just happens to have two or three finals to study for) will complain. The RAs (Resident Advisors) will respond first. They are students who are granted a certain amount of disciplinary authority by the College, but mostly they just let people into their rooms when people forget their keys and go to parties and tell people to be quiet or else "I'm going to call Campus Safety!" There is a pretty even mix between laid back and uptight RAs, and if you end up with a few of the former in your dorm, you're home free (unless of course you're one of those aforementioned people who place a high priority on sleeping and studying). Pomona's administration is generally very fair as well, and prefers everything to be handled on campus as opposed to by the police. You won't get hassled as long as you apply a modicum of common sense and courtesy.

The College Prowler® Grade on

Campus Strictness: A-

A high Campus Strictness grade implies an overall lenient atmosphere; police and RAs are fairly tolerant, and the administration's rules are flexible.

Parking

The Lowdown On...
Parking

Approximate Parking Permit Cost:
Free, but registration (required if your car isn't going to be towed) costs $30 a semester.

Pomona Parking Services:
Taken care of through campus safety
(909) 607-2000

Freshmen Allowed to Park?
Yes

Student Parking Lot?
One on South Campus and one on North Campus

Common Parking Tickets:
No Parking Zone: $20

Handicapped Zone: $100 (serves you right, you soulless beast!)

Fire Lane: $80

Did You Know?

Best Places to Find a Parking Spot
North Campus, by the library

Good Luck Getting a Parking Spot Here!
Any of the main lots during peak hours

Students Speak Out On...
Parking

{ **"Anyone can have cars, pretty much. There could be more spots to park, but compared to other schools, it's pretty good."**

 "There is **always parking available** on campus. It may be in a bad spot at the back of the lot, but it is available. Students from all years are allowed to bring cars; I'd guess maybe 20% or so actually do."

Q "It's **easy to find parking** at Pomona."

Q "I often find it **very difficult** to find parking."

Q "I guess **parking is fine**, but I don't have a car, and it would be silly to drive to my classes that are eight minutes away."

Q "The **parking scene is hot**, though it can be a little intimidating for a newcomer. Most people park their cars in student parking lots, but some people park on the street. Sometimes people park their cars and then sit on the hood drinking and spitting."

Q "Parking here is **heaven**! (I'm from San Francisco, where parking is hell.)"

Q "The parking scene on campus is hot. So hot. **It's so easy to park**."

Q "There's **always a spot somewhere**, but usually there is only one."

Q "There should be lots of room at Pomona, but due to construction in recent years there hasn't been very much parking. Watch out, **Campus Security loves doling out tickets**."

Q "**Parking here sucks**. The Claremont Police leave nowhere for students to park. Something definitely needs to be done."

The College Prowler Take On...
Parking

Parking at Pomona is easy, as long as you're willing to make some concessions. Generally, the student lots are full, and I mean always full. Who drives all those cars? How did they get their spots when no one can ever find a spot? These questions may remain forever unanswered. Fortunately, there is plenty of parking on campus if you're willing to give up on the prime spots. There is street parking all over campus, and there is always a spot somewhere, but it might be quite a walk from your destination (but really, on a six- by five-block campus, how bad can it be?). Parking will likely improve in the near future, as part of the problem has been construction that takes up many of the available parking spots.

Parking in the Village is a bad idea, as there are some very bizarre rules governing when it is okay and when it is not, and you will almost surely get a ticket, if you are lucky. If you're not lucky, your car will get towed, and by the time you get it to retrieve it, it very well might be stripped of all resellable parts. Don't say I didn't warn you. Campus Safety is pretty uptight about handing out tickets to parking violators, but you can't really blame them when there is plenty of parking available that people are too lazy to use. Some people swear that if you just don't register your car with Campus Security then they can give you as many parking tickets as they like, and you can just keep tearing them up. The only problem with this is that they will eventually call the police, and then your car will likely be towed, stripped, or worse. Still, some people seem able to get away with it. It's your neck.

The College Prowler® Grade on

Parking: B

A high grade in this section indicates that parking is both available and affordable, and that parking enforcement isn't overly severe.

Transportation

The Lowdown On...
Transportation

Ways to Get Around Town:

On Campus
Bike
Skateboard
Walk

Public Transportation
Foothill Transit (bus system)
200 First Street, Suite B
Claremont, CA 91711-0000
1-800-RIDE-INFO

Taxi Cabs
Bell Cab Co. (909) 391-1434
Yellow Cab (909) 622-1313

Car Rentals
Alamo, local: (909) 937-3600;
national: (800) 327-9633,
www.alamo.com

Avis, local: (909) 390-1441;
national: (800) 831-2847,
www.avis.com

Budget, local: (909) 983-9691;
national: (800) 527-0700,
www.budget.com

(Car Rentals, continued)

Enterprise: (909) 920-3635
national: (800) 736-8222,
www.enterprise.com

Hertz: (909) 937-8877;
national: (800) 654-3131,
www.hertz.com

National: (909) 937-7555;
national: (800) 227-7368,
www.nationalcar.com

Best Ways to Get Around Town

Again—walking, biking,
skateboarding. Claremont
is not exactly a booming
metropolis.

Ways to Get Out of Town:

Airport

Ontario Airport
(20 minutes away)

LAX (About 45 minutes
without traffic)

Airlines Serving Claremont

American Airlines,
(800) 433-7300,
www.americanairlines.com

Continental,
(800) 523-3273,
www.continental.com

Delta,
(800) 221-1212,
www.delta-air.com

Northwest,
(800) 225-2525,
www.nwa.com

(Airlines, continued)

Southwest,
(800) 435-9792,
www.southwest.com

TWA,
(800) 221-2000,
www.twa.com

United,
(800) 241-6522,
www.united.com

US Airways,
(800) 428-4322,
www.usairways.com

How to Get to the Airport

Cab, friend, Pomona Sagehen
Shuttle, Airport Shuttle -
(909) 625-2502

A cab ride to the airport costs
$20 to Ontario, $50+ to LAX.

Greyhound

(909) 624-4564

www.greyhound.com

The closest Greyhound depot
is located on Indian Hill
Boulevard, just south of the
I-10 freeway.

Amtrak

1-800-USA-RAIL

www.amtrak.com

The nearest Amtrak station is
located on Garey Avenue in
Pomona, about three miles
from campus. Service is
provided daily.

Travel Agent

Claremont Travel

325 Yale Ave.
Claaremont, CA 91711

(909) 621-3947

Students Speak Out On...
Transportation

"The train is good for getting into the main part of LA, but it closes early and only gets you to major downtown areas."

Q "You don't really need public transportation; there are lots of things in walking distance. If you need to go farther, like to Wal-Mart, there are **always people around who can drive you**."

Q "**Public transit is terrible**; do not rely on it. It's very inefficient and inconvenient. I have horrible stories of being stranded busless on strange street corners in LA late at night. Finally the frustration got to me and I had to buy a car."

Q "Pomona is a small town. **I just ride my skateboard**."

Q "**I've taken the bus to and from the Montclair Mall**. It just took about six times as long as it would have by car. At least having the transportation center just at the south end of campus (and a major bus stop at the railroad station three blocks away) makes the answer to the question, 'Where will I catch the bus?' obvious."

Q "Public transit **isn't really convenient**."

Q "Public transportation is **neither convenient nor good**."

Q "Well, I have a car, but judging from all the requests from people without cars to take them to, oh, I don't know, Del Taco, I would say **transit must not be that great**."

Q "Your **feet and legs** should work well."

Q "Most people know someone who has a car and is generous. Public **transportation around here is very entertaining**, but sometimes it takes a long time to get where you need to be."

Q "Public transportation **sucks**. You need a car."

The College Prowler Take On...
Transportation

You can sum up Claremont's transpo system in five words: not really all that good. Some students seem able to navigate the confusing waters of public transit, but many more get hopelessly lost, and some are probably still riding the bus today, haggard and tired, traveling from poorly marked bus stop to poorly marked bus stop, somehow getting ever farther from home. The buses are really slow and nightmarishly confusing, but the train, which is right next to campus, is very fast and easy. Unfortunately, the last train back from LA is at eight or nine at night, so unless you plan on spending the night, evenings in the city require a car.

This really is one of the most frustrating things about going to Pomona: feeling so confined and being so close to Los Angeles yet being unable to get there. It's do-able, just very frustrating and difficult, and it's generally not worth it. Cabs and the super shuttle work great for getting to the airport, but they are expensive for travel to LA. The only real answer is having your own car.

The College Prowler® Grade on

Transportation: D-

A high grade for Transportation indicates that campus buses, public buses, cabs, and rental cars are readily-available and affordable. Other determining factors include proximity to an airport and the necessity of transportation.

Weather

The Lowdown On...
Weather

Average Temperature:		Average Precipitation:	
Fall:	69 °F	Fall:	0.6 in.
Winter:	57 °F	Winter:	2.8 in.
Spring:	63 °F	Spring:	1.4 in.
Summer:	77 °F	Summer:	.04 in.

Did You Know?

The Santa Ana wind occasionally blows through the Inland Empire, and its hot breath can be felt on Pomona's campus from time to time. Why is this neat? Well, **the Santa Ana is one of the world's few ionized winds**. What's an ionized wind, you ask? A wind with an ionic charge, of course. Duh. These winds blow off of the east side of mountain ranges to the east of a coast, and somehow (I don't know how this works) pick up a very strong ionic charge. This charge actually affects the brain chemistry of all those it passes over, tending to kick brain activity into overdrive. Admissions to mental hospitals, murder, and suicide rates all increase dramatically in the wake of ionized winds such as the Santa Ana. So if a hot, dry, west-to-east wind is blowing, and people are acting a little strange, you might, for safety's sake, want to lock yourself up in your room without any sharp objects. Oh, and you should leave your shoe laces and belt outside too, just in case.

What's that smell? A common question from new students at Pomona. I'll tell you now: it's Chino. **Chino is about 15 miles from Pomona**, and it's the home to a huge stockyard. On certain days, when the wind is wrong, the rather heady scent of the stockyards descends over Pomona. These days are dreaded at Pomona, and many will forgo classes and social engagements to stay in their room and burn purifying incense and candles. Housing forbids these items, so you better be careful!

Students Speak Out On...
Weather

"Bring sandals; those are fine in all weather. Generally the warmest clothing one would need is pants and a sweatshirt."

Q "The weather is very **warm and mild**. It gets cold at the end of fall semester, but usually doesn't rain until spring semester. Even then, the total amount of days it rains during the year will probably add up to two weeks. Even on clear, hot days, though, it gets very cold at nights, since it's a desert climate."

Q "The weather is **one of the best things about Pomona**. It's pretty much warm with very little rain or humidity. Bring mostly warm-weather clothes, although we do get a few rainy spells, and sometimes it can get chilly (in the '40s)."

Q "I regret not having been prepared for Monsoon season. It happened every year that I was here and, every year, I was unprepared. As a result, for two weeks a year I looked like a drowned rat and felt decidedly cold and damp. If I had to do it all over again, **I'd bring an umbrella and rain shoes**."

Q "It is **really hot in September** and stays hot throughout the year during the daytime. However, in December and January, you might want a sweatshirt at night."

Q "Southern California is **blessed with a mild, almost Mediterranean, climate** thanks to its proximity to the Pacific Ocean and various complex global weather systems. Students needn't bring heavy jackets or extensive rain gear, but ought to be prepared for a few very hot days in late summer and cold evenings in the winter months."

Q "It's the desert. **It's dry, and thus cold at night**. Be prepared for that. But also bring a lot of clothes appropriate for hotness, both kinds."

Q "The weather at Pomona is **always gorgeous**. Bring shorts, tank tops, pants. Heavy sweaters and sweatshirts are rarely needed."

Q "It is **hot and sunny**. Bring primarily shorts and skirts and short-sleeves. A few pairs of pants, a few long-sleeves, a few sweatshirts or sweaters, and a raincoat will cover your needs for warmth."

Q "The **weather is the second-best thing about Pomona**. You should bring everything for warm weather, plus almost everything for cold weather, because it gets very cold (in the 40s) sometimes at night. Also, if you want to go camping in the desert, you will need warm clothes. There are many students who insist on wearing only flip-flops."

Q "The weather is about **as perfect as it can get**. I loved walking across sunny green fields of grass barefoot in shorts while ogling an amazing backdrop of snow-covered mountains."

Q "Oh, the weather is **fabulous**. Bring lots of T-shirts, but bring a jacket as well!"

The College Prowler Take On...
Weather

Well, it's Southern California. It's hot, dry, and smoggy, and there are almost never any clouds. Some people love this weather; some hate it. It certainly aids in achieving the coveted "year-long tan," which is something, but skin cancer is no picnic, and I've heard that living in Los Angeles is commensurate to smoking a pack of cigarettes a day due to the air quality (or, more accurately, the lack of air quality). After a while, the weather can get monotonous, and during winter it's just dry and clear all the time, but not even that warm, and because the Inland Empire is essentially a desert, it can get really cold at night. It doesn't snow, and it rains about once every few months. When it does rain, it pours. It's not unusual for the streets around Pomona to turn into raging rivers during a hard rain.

If you love rain and snow and wind and clouds and, well, weather, don't come to Pomona. You will be sad. Eventually, you may not notice the uniformly-bland lack of weather anymore, but you will still have a nagging feeling in your chest that something is missing. Many people express sorrow over not having seasons; Pomona really just has summer. Sometimes it's cold, but the leaves don't change, it doesn't rain, and the flowers are always in bloom. Some think of Pomona as the Garden of Eden. Silly people. According to my secular understanding of our creation myths, we were all cast out of there a long time ago. Plus, I bet the Garden of Eden wasn't so smoggy that you couldn't, two days out of three, see some mountains that were only five miles away. Still, the ability to go to the pool nearly year long, or the beach, or out hiking, can be very appealing. As long as you don't find the smelly, dry heat too appalling, you'll have no problem adjusting to the weather.

The College Prowler® Grade on

Weather: A

A high Weather grade designates that temperatures are mild and rarely reach extremes, that the campus tends to be sunny rather than rainy, and that weather is fairly consistent rather than unpredictable.

Report Card Summary

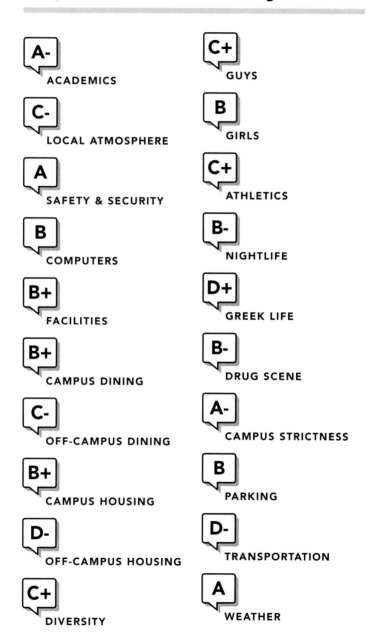

A-
ACADEMICS

C-
LOCAL ATMOSPHERE

A
SAFETY & SECURITY

B
COMPUTERS

B+
FACILITIES

B+
CAMPUS DINING

C-
OFF-CAMPUS DINING

B+
CAMPUS HOUSING

D-
OFF-CAMPUS HOUSING

C+
DIVERSITY

C+
GUYS

B
GIRLS

C+
ATHLETICS

B-
NIGHTLIFE

D+
GREEK LIFE

B-
DRUG SCENE

A-
CAMPUS STRICTNESS

B
PARKING

D-
TRANSPORTATION

A
WEATHER

Overall Experience

Students Speak Out On...
Overall Experience

"It's good. I probably would like to be in a city, but, if I could, I would put Pomona in the middle of a city, rather than attend some inferior school that's already in a city."

"I have **loved every minute of my time here**. I love the small campus and being able to see so many friends and people I know just by walking to class. The campus is gorgeous and a perfect size; small enough so you can walk everywhere easily, but large enough so that you don't feel closed in. All of the best classes I have ever taken have been during my time here. I feel like it's home, and I will genuinely miss it when I'm gone."

"**I never wanted to be anywhere else**."

Q "I really like it, and **I'm incredibly glad that I came here**. We really have it good here. Although people complain about stuff sometimes, it could be a lot worse. The school really takes care of us. We have good food, nice dorms, tons of activities, an incredibly lenient alcohol policy, and a beautiful campus. I could go on and on. The one complaint I have is that Pomona doesn't have the name recognition it should. Hopefully, guides like this one will solve that."

Q "**I seriously considered transferring or dropping out** so many times I have lost count. I was too apathetic to actually do so, however. I honestly cannot fathom how this school has earned such a favorable reputation."

Q "**I wish Pomona were in LA**. I miss being in a city. Pomona lets you have cars your freshman year, which is great, but getting in and out of LA is a pain in the rear. Other than that, I honestly could not have asked for more from a college."

Q "**I love Pomona** College. I would not want to be anywhere else."

Q "The only problem I have with Pomona right now is that **they didn't find me a job when I graduated**. Why could they not find me a job?"

Q "I **wouldn't trade my experience here for the world**. The school is all about learning how to learn. You just have to create your own experiences, and there is a lot to work with."

Q "I think Pomona was **pretty good**, but I sometimes wish I went to a school that more lay-people had heard of. It's so insulting to have paid all that money and still have people think you went to a two year community college. Alas."

The College Prowler Take On...
Overall Experience

Just about any Pomona student will tell you that they truly enjoyed their college experience. And it's not just the free booze that makes Pomona one of the happiest colleges in the country. It helps, but the booze alone couldn't make everyone so darn genuinely happy, day in and day out. After all, some people don't even drink, and they seem just as happy as everyone else. It's not the location either. The classes are good, and the professors are great, and that certainly plays its part, and it's an open, friendly campus, which is nice. But there is some other factor which makes people like this place so much. There are some people who were dead set on hating it. Why, you might wonder, did they go in the first place? One reason was parental pressure. Another was students, who by the end, had to grudgingly admit that they had enjoyed themselves. They might still claim that they don't have an affectionate place in their heart for their alma mater, but they can't deny that the experience was worthwhile.

The question is, "Why are Pomona students so unabashedly jolly?" There are only two feasible answers. One, they drug the water here. Unlikely, perhaps, but maybe Pomona is the site of a modern day governmental experiment in mass mind control. Barring that, it must be that people here just really like the people they go to college with. Are Pomona students better people than other selective liberal arts college students? Probably not. However, Pomona puts a great deal of stress on allowing people space to find their own way of doing things, both socially and academically. Sometimes, this is frustrating, sometimes people pine after the lost structure of high school and family life, but in the end, with the amount of freedom students are granted, they end up somewhere they want to be. Now if only everyone could get jobs.

The Inside Scoop

The Lowdown On...
The Inside Scoop

Pomona Slang:

Know the slang, know the school. The following is a list of things you really need to know before coming to Pomona. The more of these words you know, the better off you'll be.

The Boot – The dirty, cockroach-ridden room in which the frats hold their weekly keggers.

The Borg – Short for Oldenborg international dorm.

The Coop – The Pomona College student store, located in the Campus Center.

Forty Water – Forty ounces of malt liquor, my friend. Know it. Drink it. Love it. And don't forget to spill a drop for the dead homeys.

The Fountain – Pomona's fast food restaurant, also located in the Campus Center.

I.E. – Short for "Inland Empire," the large, deserty, trashy stretch of "civilization" to the east of LA.

→

O.E. in the I.E. – Short for "Olde English in the Inland Empire." Olde English is a fine malt liquor, O.E. in the I.E. is a practice wherein one picks a place in the Inland Empire (a petting zoo, for instance) and then goes there and drinks as much O.E. out of brown paper bags as possible.

The Quad – Short for Marston Quadrangle, the big, quadrangular grass field in the middle of Pomona campus. Also home to frequent ultimate games and a popular study spot.

Sponcest – The irreputable act of dating someone within your sponsor group.

The Towers – Tower housing units in Harwood dorm, not to be confused with the Lawry towers.

Walker Beach – A moniker for the grassy sward north of Walker Dorm. It isn't really a beach (Pomona is land locked, silly!), but it is replete with a real sand volleyball pit, and some palm trees, and lots of sunbathing students.

Walker Wall – The wall running north of Walker Beach. It is an open canvas for anyone with some art supplies and something to say. Oh heck, if you don't have anything to say, paint it anyway.

"Yo, I like you." – According to some, the best line to use when picking up prospective mates. For extra turn-on power, accompany with eyebrow twitches.

Things I Wish I Knew Before Coming to Pomona

- Not to take any classes before noon. (Though it's totally doable.)

- If you want to work with dolphins, you have to take Bio classes, Neurochem classes, Psych classes, and Cog-Sci classes. Philosophy and English don't cut it.

- Philosophy and English are fun, and they allow you, if you engage in them with vigor and verve, to be learned and yet still "cool." This lets you look down on all the naïve kids with nice haircuts and pressed pants taking computer science. All this I knew. However, what didn't occur to me is that it is these kids who get $60,000 plus job offers right out of college. Then they can afford really nice pants. Who is feeling superior now?

(Things I Wish I Knew, continued)

- Do as much stuff as possible! It is far too easy to be apathetic, both academically and socially at Pomona. Generally, the more you do, the better time you'll have.
- Dreadlocks, although tres façonable, are itchy, smelly, and generally annoying to grow.
- The King's English: It's useful, and you're not going to learn it here.

Tips to Succeed at Pomona

Butter up the professors – This may seem cheap, but most people do it, and if you want your GPA to keep up with all the other GPAs, you'd be wise to play along. This mainly applies in the humanities; in the sciences, there is somewhat more objectivity. Of course, Pomona professors are a bundle of sharp cookies (pardon my metaphor mixing), and they don't respond well to the traditional sycophant. The best way to get on their good side is to show seemingly genuine interest in their subject matter; it's generally profound and overlooked, and they want recognition as much as any of us. Then again, if you aren't interested in the subject, why are you taking it?

Decide early what you want to do and go about accomplishing it in a driven manner – It's too easy to dither away your time at Pomona, and, while this can be very pleasant, you will likely find yourself regretting that you didn't find that internship, or do that project with such and such a professor. There's always time to dither. There isn't always time to lay some serious groundwork for your future. If I took this advice back in time to my past self, I think it highly likely that my past self would deck my future self.

Pomona Urban Legends

One of Pomona's longest-standing legends centers around the group Mufti—literally meaning "undressed," the name stands for a secret society at Pomona whose sole function is to plant subversive fliers around campus. The fliers generally consist of three interrelated phrases which tend to comment on the college, its students, and society at large. Mufti-fliers are generally very convoluted and clever, and include double, triple, and even quadruple entendres making them a chore (but usually a pleasant one) to decipher.

(Urban Legends, continued)

The legend part of all this is that the only way to become part of Mufti is to catch Mufti in the act of putting up their fliers. The veracity of this legend is much debated, but I've always thought it somewhat unlikely. After all, Mufti requires a certain turn of mind, and there would be no consistency in the quality of the fliers if any old John or Jane could join up.

In the last few years, Mufti has gone even more underground, and flierings, when they occur (seldom), have been sub-par. Many think that the fliers are independently posted, and the real Mufti has disappeared, or perhaps exists in a sort of mental hibernation, just waiting for students of proper wit to come along and rouse it from its restless slumber.

Pomona Trek

Another myth regarding Pomona is that the Oldenborg dorm is the model for the ships ("cubes,") of the Borg on the television show *Star Trek*. The Borg? They are a cybernetic race of aliens who meld machine and flesh and operate in a sort of insectile collective fashion. *Star Trek*? Don't they have television on the planet you come from? Oldenborg is notoriously labyrinthine and sterile, resembling the giant cubes the Borg pilot around space.

47

Another Pomona myth is the myth of "47." This basically states that the number 47 occurs more often in nature than other integers, and that this oddity is centered around Pomona College. Of course, anyone who has taken a statistics course knows that the chances of this are slim, and it's easy to find something you're expressly looking for (yes, Pomona College is off exit 47 on the I10, but it isn't on 47th street, the 47th parallel, and so on.) However, the number 47 does hold special significance for many Pomona students. A sampling of 47 lore from the Pomona Web site:

- Pomona College is located at Exit 47 of the San Bernardino Freeway.
- The *Bible* credits Jesus with 47 miracles.
- There are 47 pipes in the top row of the Lyman Hall organ.
- The Declaration of Independence has 47 sentences.

(Urban Legends, continued)

- The Disney comedy *The Absent-Minded Professor* features a basketball game filmed at Pomona's old Renwick Gym. The final score: 47-46.
- In the film *Towering Inferno*, actor Richard Chamberlain '56 was the 47th person in line to be saved.
- In the freshman class that entered Pomona College in the year 2000, there were 47 valedictorians.
- The tropics of Cancer and Capricorn are located 47 degrees apart.

And, if all this 47 trivia gives you an upset stomach, remember that Rolaids absorbs 47 times its weight in excess acid.

I don't mean to be cynical, though. The myth of 47 is obviously redolent with whimsy. If you love whimsy, then this is the myth for you, alright. And there is a certain justificatory ironic self-awareness present in those who subscribe to it. I suppose people need a hobby to keep them off the streets.

School Spirit

Pomona students are happy, and they generally like their college, but they tend not to be all that fanatical about it. Although a disturbingly large amount of them get married on campus (generally some years after graduating; it's not that kind of school), the school is decidedly lacking in pep. People don't get that excited about sports, nor our ratings (although every time they climb, we get a little more hopeful about our prospects for getting hired). This isn't because there's anything wrong with Pomona; rather, it's just that Pomona is so laid-back. Why get worked up, people tend to think. We like our school, but we're not going to shove it down your throat.

Traditions

Birthday Dunking

It is traditional at Pomona, on the day of your birthday, that you be dunked in the Frary Courtyard fountain. Considering the number of drunken students who eject their bodily waste into this fountain on a regular basis, I always found this tradition slightly stomach turning.

Cup Drop

In Frary Dining Hall, whenever someone accidentally drops one of their plastic cups, it is customary for everyone in the dining hall to drop their cups as well (preferably empty ones, someone has to clean all that up, you know). The sound of hundreds of cups falling as one in that sonorous, cathedral-like building is deafening, and, some would claim, spiritually "moving."

Painting Walker Wall

Walker wall is a wall north of Walker dorm on North Campus. It stretches 150 some feet in a semi-circular arc, and it is the favored canvas at Pomona for anyone wishing to make a big, colorful statement to the student body. Students are allowed to paint anything they wish on the wall, and you're as likely to find a piquant bit of social commentary as you are to find a vulgar phrase (not that vulgarity doesn't have its place in piquant commentary), or just some cool pictures. The administration vows not to censor anything anybody puts on the wall, but particularly offensive messages are generally student-censored.

Ski and Beach Day

Ski and beach day is just that: a day during which participating students go skiing or snowboarding, and then hit the beach for some sun. Pomona's unique location makes this rather extravagant (and costly; it's one of the ASPCs biggest expenditures year to year) day possible.

Snow day

There isn't any snow at Pomona, but once a year a big tanker truck dumps a pile of snow on the lawn in front of the Campus Center. Snowball fights abound, but for the less rambunctious, hot chocolate is served.

Finding a Job or Internship

The Lowdown On...
Finding a Job or Internship

Pomona is a great school. However, its name-recognition factor is still sadly low. Example: Your community-college-bound high school friend asks you what school you are going to. "Pomona" you reply, full of the starry-eyed pride of the innocent. Your friend proceeds to lord it over you that you are only going to a "junior college." Such people are to be put strictly in their place, and possibly challenged to hand-to-hand combat. Employers are a different story. Engaging in fisticuffs with a prospective employer is never a good idea; if you win, they'll begrudge you and likely not make you a part of "the team." Conversely, if you lose, they'll probably remind you that "losers" don't have a place in the corporate culture of contemporary America. Fortunately for you, while Pomona's acclaim has yet to spread to the ears of your friends, it is relatively well-known by those who matter (i.e., matter apropos hiring; your friends matter too, I'm sure. But they probably aren't going to hire you.)

Advice

Don't be afraid to go to the Career Center; the employees are extremely nice and awfully eager to help you (it's their job). The earlier you hit this place up the better off you'll be when your magical four years finally draw to a close, and you realize that you're going to turn into a pumpkin (not a very employable pumpkin.)

Take internships! They are easy enough to get if you talk to professors and people in the Career Center, and they will not only break up your college routine (very good thing, sometimes), but they will give you something to put on your resume other than "college."

Establish rapport with and work with professors; you never know when they might be able to hook you up, and many of them are fine, interesting people to boot.

Career Center Resources & Services

Career Development Office (909) 621-8144
www.Pomona.edu/cdo/

The CDO offers:

• Access to the Alumni Database

• Career Fairs

• Job Counseling

• Resume Workshops

Firms That Most Frequently Hire Graduates

Americorps, Analysis Group/Economics, AT&T, Bain and Company, Barrington Associates, Bear Stearns, Bonne, Bridges, Mueller, O'Keefe & Nichols, Calprig, Cambridge Associates, Campaign to Save the Enviroment, City of Hope Medical Center, Dept. of Justice, Deutsche Bank, Exploration Summer Programs, Federal Reserve Bank, Gallo Winery, Georgetown University, Green Corps, Harvard, IMG, JET, LAUSD, Lazard LLC, Lehman Brothers, Merril Lynch, NYC Public Schools, Peace Corps, Pitney Bowes, Teach for America, US State Dept., UESF Aids Health Project, Wellpoint, Wells Fargo

Average Salary Information

Business	$35,000–$80,000
Education	$21,000–$40,000
Law and Government	$32,000–$37,000
Non-Profit	$9,000–$20,000 (with room and board)
Research	$27,000–$35,000

Career Summary

If you want a good job right out of the gate, study economics or computer science, and try to get some internships while you're in school. Then, when you're a junior or senior, spit-shine your shoes and go to the career fair with some nice clothes and you'll land a good job. It's a sure thing. However, if this just isn't what you want to do, it's not so easy. Pomona is respected, and we have a powerful alumni base, but one of the downfalls (maybe it's a benefit too) of the liberal arts education is that it doesn't prepare you to do one thing well; rather, it prepares you to be good at preparing to do anything. This means that your work isn't over after college. You better be ready, is all I have to say, because most Pomona students don't get their dream job on a platter. However, if you check out the number of Pomona students with jobs in the arts, politics, journalism, etc., it's pretty clear that a lot of students do get their dream jobs. It just takes time.

Alumni

The Lowdown On...
Alumni

Web Site:
www.Pomona.edu/Alumni/
Home.shtml

Services Available:
Online Alumni Database

Office:
Office of Alumni Relations
The Seaver House
305 N. College Ave.
Claremont, CA 91711

Major Alumni Events

Alumni weekend – A weekend where all Pomona alums are encouraged to return to Pomona and kick it one more time, college style.

Mug passing – A ceremony wherein Pomona alums pass mugs to new Pomona freshmen

Alumni Publications

The New York Times (no, not really, but alum Bill Keller is the new Editor-in-Chief). The Alumni does not have an official publication, but you can keep track of what's happening in the Pomona-alum world by visiting the Web site.

Did You Know?

Famous Pomona Alums

John Cage – avant garde composer

Kris Kristofferson – Actor; is he famous for anything other than that Janis Joplin song, "Bobby McGee?" (maybe not, but he was a Rhodes scholar)

James Turrell – artist

Tom Waits – singer songwriter

Student Organizations

There are more than 400 student organizations on campus. The following is a partial list:

Arts Organizations

Claremont Colleges' Ballroom Dance

Collaborative Productions, film production group

Pomona College Student Art Gallery (PoSA)

Film Society

Without a Box, improvisational theatre group

Communications

Collage, five-college newsmagazine

Harmony, multicultural newspaper

KSPC-FM, radio station

Las Voices Unidas, Latino student newspaper

Metate, yearbook

Pacific Winds, Asian/Pacific Islander newspaper

The Re-View, feminist newspaper

The Spectator, literary magazine

The Student Life, Pomona College newspaper

Honor Societies

Mortar Board

Phi Beta Kappa

Sigma Xi

Musical Organizations

Pomona College Choir

Pomona College Concert Band

Pomona College Glee Club

Pomona College Gospel Choir

Pomona College Orchestra

Chamber Ensembles

Jazz Ensemble

Men's and Women's Blue and White (a cappella singing groups)

Musicians' Guild

Students for the Preservation of Acoustic Music

Shades (a cappella singing group)

Political Groups

ACT!

Amnesty International

Asian American Student Alliance

Central American Concern

Claremont Colleges Democratic Club

Claremont Colleges Republicans

International Relations Colloquium

Model United Nations

Peace Through Justice

Student Association for the Environment (SAFE)

Religious Groups

Baha'i Club

Christian Science Organization

Pathfinder (Five-College Christian Fellowship)

Hillel-Jewish Fellowship

InterVarsity Christian Fellowship

Service Organizations

CARE

Community Interaction Fund Committee

Habitat for Humanity

Student Volunteers for the American Red Cross

Volunteer Services

Volunteers for Youth

World Hunger Coalition

Special Interest Groups

Admissions Tour Guides/Hosts

After Hours Cafe

Association International des Etudiantes des Sciences Economique et Commercial (AIESEC)

Association for Women in Science

Bridge Club

Capoeira Club

College Bowl

Economics Club

Five-College Women's Coalition

Forensics Society

Fraternities

International Club

Lesbian, Gay, and Bisexual Students Union

Mathematics Club

Minority Student Action Program

On the Loose, hiking and climbing club

Organization of Pre-Health Students

PALS

Racial Awareness and Cultural Experience (R.A.C.E.)

Racquetball Club

Recycling Action Committee

Scuba Club

Ski Club

Society for Creative Anachronism

(Special Interest Groups, continued)

Student AIDS Awareness Committee

Student Health Advisory Committee

Women's Union

Irish American Society

Islamic Society

Student Government

Associated Students of Pomona College (ASPC)

ASPC Senate

Club Sports Council

Committee for Intramural Sports

Dormitory President's Council

Five-College President's Council

Five-College Social Affairs Committee

Student-Faculty Interaction Committee

Cultural

The Best
& Worst

The Ten BEST Things About Pomona

1	The caring and nurturing environment. Oh, yeah, and did I mention the free beer?
2	Climbing the flag pole
3	Free strawberry-flavored condoms!
4	Table Manners
5	Sneaking into Frary
6	Rolling in on the frat boys and then ganking their booze
7	Impromptu rock and roll concerts in the campus center
8	The streets flow with free beer
9	Grade inflation (when it benefits you)
10	Three words: Delhi Palace Express

The Ten **WORST** Things About Pomona

1 Claremont

2 Chino winds

3 The network going down when, and only when, it is most inconvenient

4 Fusty old Claremont residents spoiling our good, clean, and maybe sometimes a little bit noisy fun

5 The international dining hall in Oldenborg

6 Grade inflation (when it benefits everyone else)

7 8:20 a.m. classes

8 Quiet hours

9 The mailroom after afternoon classes

10 Baxter Health Center

Visiting

The Lowdown On...

Visiting

Hotel Information:

Claremont Inn
555 West Foothill Blvd.
(909) 626-2411
Distance from Campus:
1.5 miles
Price Range: $80–$120

Claremont Lodge
736 S Indian Hill Blvd.
(909) 626-5654
Ditsance from Campus:
1.5 miles
Price Range: $50–$70

Hotel Claremont
840 S Indian Hill Blvd.
(909) 621-4831
Distance from Campus:
1.5 miles
Price Range: $70–$100

Take a Campus Virtual Tour

Go to *www.Pomona.edu/tours*

To Schedule a Group Information Session or Interview

During the school year, information sessions are held Monday through Friday at 11 a.m., and in the summer they are offered at 10 a.m. From mid-September through the beginning of December, information sessions are also held on Saturdays at noon, except Thanksgiving weekend. Contact admissions just verify the date and time just to make sure. Call to schedule an interview, which is highly recommended.

Pomona College

Office of Admissions

333 N College Way
Claremont, CA 91711-6312

(909) 621-8134

admissions@Pomona.edu

www.pomona.edu/admissions

Campus Tours

Sign up with the admissions office and bring your parents, too! Tours are available on most weekdays.

Overnight Visits

If you visit Pomona during the school year, you can stay overnight with a student in the dorms. Just call the Office of Admissions to schedule the visit and find out more about what you'll do and what you should bring. You could also attend a Pomona class in the morning, so you'll want to be prepared.

Directions to Campus

Driving from the North

- Take I-5 South to the I-10 East
- Exit at Indian Hill Boulevard, drive north one mile, take a right on Bonita Avenue and the Admissions Office parking lot is four blocks down on your left

Driving from the South

- Take the 57 North to the I-10 East
- Exit at Indian Hill Boulevard, drive north one mile, take a right on Bonita Avenue and the Admissions Office parking lot is four blocks down on your left

Driving from the East

- Take the I-10 West
- Exit at Indian Hill Boulevard, drive north one mile, take a right on Bonita Avenue and the Admissions Office parking lot is four blocks down on your left

Driving from the West

- Take the I-10 East
- Exit at Indian Hill Boulevard, drive north one mile, take a right on Bonita Avenue and the Admissions Office parking lot is four blocks down on your left

Words to Know

Academic Probation – A suspension imposed on a student if he or she fails to keep up with the school's minimum academic requirements. Those unable to improve their grades after receiving this warning can face dismissal.

Beer Pong/Beirut – A drinking game involving cups of beer arranged in a pyramid shape on each side of a table. The goal is to get a ping pong ball into one of the opponent's cups by throwing the ball or hitting it with a paddle. If the ball lands in a cup, the opponent is required to drink the beer.

Bid – An invitation from a fraternity or sorority to 'pledge' (join) that specific house.

Blue-Light Phone – Brightly-colored phone posts with a blue light bulb on top. These phones exist for security purposes and are located at various outside locations around most campuses. In an emergency, a student can pick up one of these phones (free of charge) to connect with campus police or a security escort.

Campus Police – Police who are specifically assigned to a given institution. Campus police are typically not regular city officers; they are employed by the university in a full-time capacity.

Club Sports – A level of sports that falls somewhere between varsity and intramural. If a student is unable to commit to a varsity team but has a lot of passion for athletics, a club sport could be a better, less intense option. Even less demanding, intramural (IM) sports often involve no traveling and considerably less time.

Cocaine – An illegal drug. Also known as "coke" or "blow," cocaine often resembles a white crystalline or powdery substance. It is highly addictive and dangerous.

Common Application – An application with which students can apply to multiple schools.

Course Registration – The period of official class selection for the upcoming quarter or semester. Prior to registration, it is best to prepare several back-up courses in case a particular class becomes full. If a course is full, students can place themselves on the waitlist, although this still does not guarantee entry.

Division Athletics – Athletic classifications range from Division I to Division III. Division IA is the most competitive, while Division III is considered to be the least competitive.

Dorm – A dorm (or dormitory) is an on-campus housing facility. Dorms can provide a range of options from suite-style rooms to more communal options that include shared bathrooms. Most first-year students live in dorms. Some upperclassmen who wish to stay on campus also choose this option.

Early Action – An application option with which a student can apply to a school and receive an early acceptance response without a binding commitment. This system is becoming less and less available.

Early Decision – An application option that students should use only if they are certain they plan to attend the school in question. If a student applies using the early decision option and is admitted, he or she is required and bound to attend that university. Admission rates are usually higher among students who apply through early decision, as the student is clearly indicating that the school is his or her first choice.

Ecstasy – An illegal drug. Also known as "E" or "X," ecstasy looks like a pill and most resembles an aspirin. Considered a party drug, ecstasy is very dangerous and can be deadly.

Ethernet – An extremely fast Internet connection available in most university-owned residence halls. To use an Ethernet connection properly, a student will need a network card and cable for his or her computer.

Fake ID – A counterfeit identification card that contains false information. Most commonly, students get fake IDs with altered birthdates so that they appear to be older than 21 (and therefore of legal drinking age). Even though it is illegal, many college students have fake IDs in hopes of purchasing alcohol or getting into bars.

Frosh – Slang for "freshman" or "freshmen."

Hazing – Initiation rituals administered by some fraternities or sororities as part of the pledging process. Many universities have outlawed hazing due to its degrading, and sometimes dangerous, nature.

Intramurals (IMs) – A popular, and usually free, sport league in which students create teams and compete against one another. These sports vary in competitiveness and can include a range of activities—everything from billiards to water polo. IM sports are a great way to meet people with similar interests.

Keg – Officially called a half-barrel, a keg contains roughly 200 12-ounce servings of beer.

LSD – An illegal drug, also known as acid, this hallucinogenic drug most commonly resembles a tab of paper.

Marijuana – An illegal drug, also known as weed or pot; along with alcohol, marijuana is one of the most commonly-found drugs on campuses across the country.

Major –The focal point of a student's college studies; a specific topic that is studied for a degree. Examples of majors include physics, English, history, computer science, economics, business, and music. Many students decide on a specific major before arriving on campus, while others are simply "undecided" until declaring a major. Those who are extremely interested in two areas can also choose to double major.

Meal Block – The equivalent of one meal. Students on a meal plan usually receive a fixed number of meals per week. Each meal, or "block," can be redeemed at the school's dining facilities in place of cash. Often, a student's weekly allotment of meal blocks will be forfeited if not used.

Minor – An additional focal point in a student's education. Often serving as a complement or addition to a student's main area of focus, a minor has fewer requirements and prerequisites to fulfill than a major. Minors are not required for graduation from most schools; however some students who want to explore many different interests choose to pursue both a major and a minor.

Mushrooms – An illegal drug. Also known as "'shrooms," this drug resembles regular mushrooms but is extremely hallucinogenic.

Off-Campus Housing – Housing from a particular landlord or rental group that is not affiliated with the university. Depending on the college, off-campus housing can range from extremely popular to non-existent. Students who choose to live off campus are typically given more freedom, but they also have to deal with possible subletting scenarios, furniture, bills, and other issues. In addition to these factors, rental prices and distance often affect a student's decision to move off campus.

Office Hours – Time that teachers set aside for students who have questions about coursework. Office hours are a good forum for students to go over any problems and to show interest in the subject material.

Pledging – The early phase of joining a fraternity or sorority, pledging takes place after a student has gone through rush and received a bid. Pledging usually lasts between one and two semesters. Once the pledging period is complete and a particular student has done everything that is required to become a member, that student is considered a brother or sister. If a fraternity or a sorority would decide to "haze" a group of students, this initiation would take place during the pledging period.

Private Institution – A school that does not use tax revenue to subsidize education costs. Private schools typically cost more than public schools and are usually smaller.

Prof – Slang for "professor."

Public Institution – A school that uses tax revenue to subsidize education costs. Public schools are often a good value for in-state residents and tend to be larger than most private colleges.

Quarter System (or Trimester System) – A type of academic calendar system. In this setup, students take classes for three academic periods. The first quarter usually starts in late September or early October and concludes right before Christmas. The second quarter usually starts around early to mid–January and finishes up around March or April. The last academic quarter, or "third quarter," usually starts in late March or early April and finishes up in late May or Mid-June. The fourth quarter is summer. The major difference between the quarter system and semester system is that students take more, less comprehensive courses under the quarter calendar.

RA (Resident Assistant) – A student leader who is assigned to a particular floor in a dormitory in order to help to the other students who live there. An RA's duties include ensuring student safety and providing assistance wherever possible.

Recitation – An extension of a specific course; a review session. Some classes, particularly large lectures, are supplemented with mandatory recitation sessions that provide a relatively personal class setting.

Rolling Admissions – A form of admissions. Most commonly found at public institutions, schools with this type of policy continue to accept students throughout the year until their class sizes are met. For example, some schools begin accepting students as early as December and will continue to do so until April or May.

Room and Board – This figure is typically the combined cost of a university-owned room and a meal plan.

Room Draw/Housing Lottery – A common way to pick on-campus room assignments for the following year. If a student decides to remain in university-owned housing, he or she is assigned a unique number that, along with seniority, is used to determine his or her housing for the next year.

Rush – The period in which students can meet the brothers and sisters of a particular chapter and find out if a given fraternity or sorority is right for them. Rushing a fraternity or a sorority is not a requirement at any school. The goal of rush is to give students who are serious about pledging a feel for what to expect.

Semester System – The most common type of academic calendar system at college campuses. This setup typically includes two semesters in a given school year. The fall semester starts around the end of August or early September and concludes before winter vacation. The spring semester usually starts in mid-January and ends in late April or May.

Student Center/Rec Center/Student Union – A common area on campus that often contains study areas, recreation facilities, and eateries. This building is often a good place to meet up with fellow students; depending on the school, the student center can have a huge role or a non-existent role in campus life.

Student ID – A university-issued photo ID that serves as a student's key to school-related functions. Some schools require students to show these cards in order to get into dorms, libraries, cafeterias, and other facilities. In addition to storing meal plan information, in some cases, a student ID can actually work as a debit card and allow students to purchase things from bookstores or local shops.

Suite – A type of dorm room. Unlike dorms that feature communal bathrooms shared by the entire floor, suites offer bathrooms shared only among the suite. Suite-style dorm rooms can house anywhere from two to ten students.

TA (Teacher's Assistant) – An undergraduate or grad student who helps in some manner with a specific course. In some cases, a TA will teach a class, assist a professor, grade assignments, or conduct office hours.

Undergraduate – A student in the process of studying for his or her bachelor's degree.

ABOUT THE AUTHOR

I am a recent graduate of Pomona College. No, I do not have a high paying job yet. Yet. However, I plan to use the fame I garner from authoring this guide to jump-start my plans for world-pop-cultural domination, and fame is better than money any day. It's a lofty goal, but when you wish upon a star ... I envision myself being sort of a genetically spliced version of Donald Barthelme, Ludwig Wittgenstein, and Lou Reed. Sort of like the bastard child of higher education and pop culture. I am moving to New York where, hopefully, I will learn to "hob-nob," and then meet and wow all sorts of high-powered editors. Then I will use my new, "phat" connections to score some book rights. See? I already speak the "lingo." Currently, I'm working on a sort of modern spin-off of Don Juan. It's not like the one with Marlon Brando and Johnny Depp, where at the end Marlon Brando tries to dance with his wife, but can't because he is just too big. It's more like what I think Lord Byron would write if he were alive and kicking today. Oh, and the rhyme scheme is the same as in Don Juan, which I think is an atavistic, but just-in-the-right-sort-of-way-to-be-considered-bold kind of move.

If those plans flop, I am thinking of becoming an underwear model. I've got the abs, but I don't know how to break into the business. Oh, I also want to work with dolphins. As of yet, I've been unable to think of a way to meld my three career choices. Ooh, ooh! I also want to be a modern day pirate. Unfortuantely, Pomona didn't offer a degree in bucaneering. However, I have boundless faith in my own ability to adjust my desires to match the likely-peripatetic route my life will probably end up taking.

Oh yeah, before I forget, here are my promised shout outs: Colin, Aimee, Claire, Krista, Eve, and..., oh crud, I can't remember the rest of you. So I reneged on my promise to recognize you. What are you going to do about it?

I'd like to thank my parents for putting me up while I was writing this, but I won't, because they told me to save my thanks for when I win the Pulitzer, or something else that won't "embarrass" them. Oh yeah, but I will say "hey" to Lilas. She's my girlfriend. At least, at the time of my writing this she is. Who knows what the future may hold. Gosh, that would be sort of funny if we're not together anymore when this book gets published. Wait … now I'm thinking I shouldn't have got that tattoo either. Oh well. Lilas, if you're reading this and we're still together, I dedicate this, my first book, to you. Oh what the heck. If we broke up, I'm still dedicating it to you. Merry Christmas. But only if I broke up with you. If you broke up with me, than this book is dedicated to my future girlfriend, whoever she may be.

Peter Cook
petercook@collegeprowler.com

California Colleges

California dreamin'?
This book is a must have for you!

CALIFORNIA COLLEGES
7¼" X 10", 762 Pages Paperback
$29.95 Retail
1-59658-501-3

Stanford, UC Berkeley, Caltech—California is home
to some of America's greatest institutes of higher
learning. *California Colleges* gives the lowdown on 24
of the best, side by side, in one prodigious volume.

New England Colleges

Looking for peace in the Northeast?
Pick up this regional guide to New England!

NEW ENGLAND COLLEGES
7¼" X 10", 1015 Pages Paperback
$29.95 Retail
1-59658-504-8

New England is the birthplace of many prestigious universities, and with so many to choose from, picking the right school can be a tough decision. With inside information on over 34 competive Northeastern schools, *New England Colleges* provides the same high-quality information prospective students expect from College Prowler in one all-inclusive, easy-to-use reference.

Schools of the South

Headin' down south? This book will help you find your way to the perfect school!

SCHOOLS OF THE SOUTH
7¼" X 10", 773 Pages Paperback
$29.95 Retail
1-59658-503-X

Southern pride is always strong. Whether it's across town or across state, many Southern students are devoted to their home sweet home. *Schools of the South* offers an honest student perspective on 36 universities available south of the Mason-Dixon.

Untangling
the Ivy League

The ultimate book for everything Ivy!

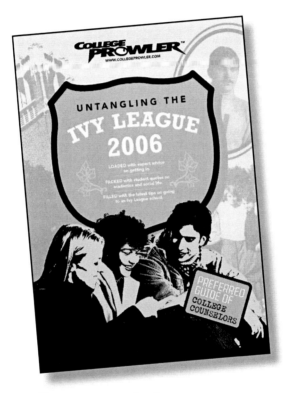

UNTANGLING THE IVY LEAGUE
7¼" X 10", 567 Pages Paperback
$24.95 Retail
1-59658-500-5

Ivy League students, alumni, admissions officers,
and other top insiders get together to tell it like it is.
Untangling the Ivy League covers every aspect—from
admissions and athletics to secret societies and urban
legends—of the nation's eight oldest, wealthiest, and
most competitive colleges and universities.

Need Help Paying For School?

Apply for our scholarship!

College Prowler awards thousands of dollars a year
to students who compose the best essays.
E-mail scholarship@collegeprowler.com for more
information, or call 1-800-290-2682.

Apply now at *www.collegeprowler.com*

Tell Us What Life Is Really Like at Your School!

Have you ever wanted to let people know what your college is really like? Now's your chance to help millions of high school students choose the right college.

Let your voice be heard.

Check out **www.collegeprowler.com** for more info!

Need More Help?

Do you have more questions about this school? Can't find a certain statistic? College Prowler is here to help. We are the best source of college information out there. We have a network of thousands of students who can get the latest information on any school to you ASAP. E-mail us at info@collegeprowler.com with your college-related questions.

E-Mail Us Your College-Related Questions!

Check out **www.collegeprowler.com** for more details.
1-800-290-2682

Write For Us!
Get published! Voice your opinion.

Writing a College Prowler guidebook is both fun and rewarding; our open-ended format allows your own creativity free reign. Our writers have been featured in national newspapers and have seen their names in bookstores across the country. Now is your chance to break into the publishing industry with one of the country's fastest-growing publishers!

Apply now at ***www.collegeprowler.com***

Contact editor@collegeprowler.com or
call 1-800-290-2682 for more details.

Pros and Cons

Still can't figure out if this is the right school for you?
You've already read through this in-depth guide; why not
list the pros and cons? It will really help with narrowing down
your decision and determining whether or not
this school is right for you.

Pros	Cons
....	....
....	....
....	....
....	....
....	....
....	....
....	....
....	....
....	....
....	....
....	....
....	....

Pros and Cons

Still can't figure out if this is the right school for you?
You've already read through this in-depth guide; why not
list the pros and cons? It will really help with narrowing down
your decision and determining whether or not
this school is right for you.

Pros	Cons
....	....
....	....
....	....
....	....
....	....
....	....
....	....
....	....
....	....
....	....
....	....
....	....
....	....

Notes

....

....

....

....

....

....

....

....

....

....

....

....

....

Notes

....

....

....

....

....

....

....

....

....

....

....

....

....

Notes

....

....

....

....

....

....

....

....

....

....

....

....

....

Notes

....

....

....

....

....

....

....

....

....

....

....

....

....

Notes

....

....

....

....

....

....

....

....

....

....

....

....

....

Notes

....

....

....

....

....

....

....

....

....

....

....

....

....

Notes

....

....

....

....

....

....

....

....

....

....

....

....

....

Notes

....

....

....

....

....

....

....

....

....

....

....

....

....

....

Notes

....

....

....

....

....

....

....

....

....

....

....

....

....

Notes

....

....

....

....

....

....

....

....

....

....

....

....

....

Notes

....

....

....

....

....

....

....

....

....

....

....

....

....

Notes

....

....

....

....

....

....

....

....

....

....

....

....

....

....

Notes

....

....

....

....

....

....

....

....

....

....

....

....

....

Notes

....

....

....

....

....

....

....

....

....

....

....

....

....

Notes

....
....
....
....
....
....
....
....
....
....
....
....
....

Notes

....

....

....

....

....

....

....

....

....

....

....

....

....

Notes

....

....

....

....

....

....

....

....

....

....

....

....

....

Notes

....

....

....

....

....

....

....

....

....

....

....

....

....

Notes

....

....

....

....

....

....

....

....

....

....

....

....

....

Notes

....

....

....

....

....

....

....

....

....

....

....

....

....

Notes

....

....

....

....

....

....

....

....

....

....

....

....

....

Notes

....

....

....

....

....

....

....

....

....

....

....

....

....

Notes

....

....

....

....

....

....

....

....

....

....

....

....

....

Notes

....

....

....

....

....

....

....

....

....

....

....

....

....

Notes

....

....

....

....

....

....

....

....

....

....

....

....

....

....